Learning
Unlimited

Learning
Unlimited

Strategies for
Students with
Limited or
Interrupted
Formal
Education
and Other Struggling
Multilingual Learners

Nicoleta Filimon
Christi Cartwright-Lacerda

 ascd   Arlington, Virginia USA

2800 Shirlington Rd., Suite 1001 • Arlington, VA 22206 USA

Phone: 800-933-2723 or 703-578-9600 • Fax: 703-575-5400

Website: www.ascd.org • Email: member@ascd.org

Author guidelines: www.ascd.org/write

Richard Culatta, *Chief Executive Director;* Anthony Rebora, *Chief Content Officer;* Genny Ostertag, *Managing Director, Book Acquisitions and Editing;* Susan Hills, *Senior Acquisitions Editor;* Mary Beth Nielsen, *Director, Book Editing;* Jamie Greene, *Senior Editor;* Beth Schlenoff, *Graphic Designer;* Valerie Younkin, *Senior Production Designer;* Kelly Marshall, *Production Manager;* Christopher Logan, *Senior Production Specialist;* Kathryn Oliver, *Creative Project Manager;* Shajuan Martin, *E-Publishing Specialist*

All web links in this book are correct as of the publication date below but may have become inactive or otherwise modified since that time. If you notice a deactivated or changed link, please email books@ascd.org with the words "Link Update" in the subject line. In your message, please specify the web link, the book title, and the page number on which the link appears.

PAPERBACK ISBN: 978-1-4166-3312-9   ASCD product #124010   n11/24

PDF EBOOK ISBN: 978-1-4166-3313-6; see Books in Print for other formats.

Quantity discounts are available: email programteam@ascd.org or call 800-933-2723, ext. 5773, or 703-575-5773. For desk copies, go to www.ascd.org/deskcopy.

Library of Congress Cataloging-in-Publication Data

Names: Filimon, Nicoleta, author. | Cartwright-Lacerda, Christi, author.

Title: Learning unlimited : strategies for students with limited or interrupted formal education and other struggling multilingual learners / Nicoleta Filimon & Christi Cartwright-Lacerda.

Description: Arlington, Virginia USA : ASCD, [2025] | Includes bibliographical references and index.

Identifiers: LCCN 2024030023 (print) | LCCN 2024030024 (ebook) | ISBN 9781416633129 (paperback) | ISBN 9781416633136 (adobe pdf) | ISBN 9781416633518 (epub)

Subjects: LCSH: Education, Bilingual—United States. | Immigrants—Education—United States. | Refugees—United States—Social conditions. | English language—Study and teaching— Foreign speakers. | Literacy—Study and teaching—United States. | Multicultural education.

Classification: LCC LC3731 .F495 2025 (print) | LCC LC3731 (ebook) | DDC 370.117/50973—dc23/ eng/20240926

LC record available at https://lccn.loc.gov/2024030023

LC ebook record available at https://lccn.loc.gov/2024030024

31 30 29 28 27 26 25   1 2 3 4 5 6 7 8 9 10 11 12

Learning Unlimited

"We pass through this world but once. Few tragedies can be more extensive than the stunting of life, few injustices deeper than the denial of an opportunity to strive or even to hope, by a limit imposed from without, but falsely identified as lying within."

—Stephen Jay Gould, *The Mismeasure of Man*

Acknowledgments

To make this book a reality would not be possible without the support of some very special people we would like to take this moment to thank. First of all, we'd like to thank Geraldo, Laurie, Heidi, and Meghan for their unwavering belief and confidence in us. To our editors, Susan and Jamie, and the wonderful team at ASCD, we are eternally grateful for your willingness to take a chance on us. Your steady guidance and vast expertise have made the process of publishing this book so rewarding. A big thank you to our past and present colleagues and friends who have provided guidance and encouragement when it was most needed.

Christi would like to extend her deep gratitude to Nicoleta who was her mentor when she first began teaching. Nicoleta's determination, strength, and commitment to all students, especially SLIFE, serve as an example for all educators to aspire to. Christi would like to extend a special thanks to her mom for always believing in her and supporting her as both a student and teacher. Her values of hard work, responsibility, and the importance of education will never be forgotten. Christi would like to especially thank her husband, Gustavo, for his faith in her and her dream to write a book. It was Gustavo who helped Christi land her first ELD teaching position in Vila Velha, Brazil, which led to a lifelong career path in education. Christi extends her heartfelt thanks to the two little learners who inspire her most: Gabriella and Leonardo. Christi would also like to extend her thanks to her sister and brother, Melissa and Jason, for their invaluable support.

Nicoleta would like to express her deepest gratitude to her mother, Marica, a retired elementary school teacher, who first inspired her to become an educator. It was in her mother's 2nd grade classroom in Romania where Nicoleta, who was completing her student practicum at the time, discovered a very important lesson: teaching, as well as learning, cannot flourish in the absence of compassion. It was this lesson, as well as her mother's lifelong commitment to underserved students, that Nicoleta tries to remember every time she teaches her students. Nicoleta would like to extend a special thanks to her husband, Marcel, and their daughter, Julia, her biggest fans, for always believing in her and for being there every time she stumbled. There are no words to express how much she appreciates their endless supply of enthusiasm and energy. Nicoleta would also like to thank Christi, her friend and colleague, for her unwavering support over the years. A big thank you goes to her father, Nicolae; her sisters, Amalia and Malina; and her in-laws, Cornelia and Iacob, for their encouragement.

Introduction: Understanding the Struggles of Students with Limited or Interrupted Formal Education and Other Multilingual Learners

As teachers of students with limited or interrupted formal education (SLIFE) and struggling multilingual learners (MLs), we are very familiar with the obstacles educators encounter when trying to meet the needs of their students. Our students are your students, too. They include teenagers mismatched with elementary-style curricular resources, high school–aged newcomers deemed not making progress despite significant gains, and exhausted wage earners falling asleep in class after working a night shift. This book is designed to equip teachers with practical solutions catering to the needs of these very students. We outline strategies that we have found effective as well as an instructional model that addresses the needs of SLIFE and other struggling MLs. Each strategy is accompanied by sample instructional materials and templates meant to be used or to serve as inspiration for creating your own. Our book sets out to answer the most pressing question that teachers ask themselves: What strategies can I use in my daily instruction to meet the needs of my students?

With an increasing number of MLs in our schools, it has become apparent that many of them struggle to meet grade-level expectations.

This is especially true for newcomers and SLIFE. Newcomers are broadly defined by the U.S. Department of Education as "K–12 students born outside the United States who have arrived in the country in the last three years and are still learning English" (2023, p. 4). Factors such as home language literacy, degree of prior schooling, and migration history can all serve as obstacles to meeting educational demands (Institute of Education Sciences, 2018). Due to language barriers and work schedules, family and caregiver engagement can also be a struggle.

A subset of the ML population, SLIFE are students with limited literacy skills in their native language and who are below grade level in most academic skills (Freeman & Freeman, 2002). Although statistics on the current number of SLIFE in U.S. schools are not available, Fleischman and Hopstock (1993) estimated that 20 percent of high school MLs and 12 percent of middle school MLs had missed two or more years of schooling (as cited in Ruiz de Velasco & Fix, 2000). In a more recent study, Potochnick (2018) found that 11.4 percent of foreign-born 10th graders had arrived in the United States with interrupted schooling.

As SLIFE and other struggling MLs enroll in U.S. schools, they confront a plethora of challenges that interfere—in some cases quite significantly—with their ability to acquire language and content and meet grade-level expectations. As DeCapua and colleagues (2007) note, many SLIFE have faced issues such as "war, migration, lack of education facilities, cultural dictates, and economic circumstances" (p. 40). Montero and colleagues (2014) underscore that in many cases, SLIFE have experienced years "without access to the foundations of formal education—literacy and numeracy" (p. 59). According to Wright (2015), many SLIFE have encountered discrimination and were systematically denied access to education in their native countries.

Because of their limited or interrupted schooling experiences, SLIFE often possess minimal or even nonexistent literacy skills in their native language (Custodio & O'Loughlin, 2020; DeCapua & Marshall, 2015; DeCapua et al., 2007; Freeman & Freeman, 2002; Montero et al., 2014;

Windle & Miller, 2012). Consequently, these students lack sufficient or accurate background knowledge related to academic concepts, possess limited academic vocabulary in their native language, and have inadequate exposure to various literary genres (DeCapua & Marshall, 2015; Montero et al., 2014; Windle & Miller, 2012). This reality puts SLIFE at a significant disadvantage since, upon enrolling in U.S. schools, they face the additional challenges of learning English, becoming proficient in a prescribed set of knowledge and skills, and preparing for high-stakes assessments (DeCapua et al., 2009).

We see these issues brought to life every day by the students in our classrooms. For example, consider Luis, a 17-year-old SLIFE enrolled in 9th grade. Luis always arrives to class on time and is eager to copy down the opening activity, often meticulously using colored pens and pencils to re-create any colored or bolded fonts. But when it comes to completing a prompt with a response of his own, he stops. Though Luis can easily list everything he sees in the pictures accompanying our text, he is unable to make inferences from the list.

Like Luis, Yakaury, a 16-year-old who recently immigrated to the United States, has a hard time making inferences even when provided with scaffolds such as pictures, sentence stems, or native-language supports. She can easily provide answers to factual questions that require her to look for keywords in the text and copy text parts to support her answers, but she has difficulty dealing with higher-order questions whose answers cannot be readily gleaned from the text.

And then there's Amauris. Though he has spent two years in our program, he's unfortunately made little academic progress. His literacy skills in both English and his home language are even less developed than those of his classmates. Unlike most of his peers, who work diligently on the tasks assigned, he would rather act up in class than reveal his academic struggles. The only time he is willing to participate is after hearing his peers' answers, which he is able to memorize.

Obstacles Faced by SLIFE and Other Struggling MLs

In addition to the obstacles that the research and student experiences reveal, SLIFE often confront "cultural dissonance," which is defined as a "mismatch between home and school" (DeCapua & Marshall, 2011a, p. 25). This mismatch occurs as SLIFE encounter different cultural values and become acquainted with a different learning paradigm in U.S. schools. This learning paradigm is predicated on the future relevance of the taught curriculum, student independence, individual accountability, dependence on the written word, and analytical academic tasks, such as classifying, comparing and contrasting, and synthesizing. On the other hand, many SLIFE come from environments that emphasize the immediate relevance of knowledge, interconnectedness, shared responsibility, oral transmission of information, and pragmatic tasks focused on real-world applications (DeCapua & Marshall, 2011a). The cultural dissonance that SLIFE experience can therefore have detrimental effects on their academic performance, resulting in low academic achievement and high dropout rates.

Immigration status can also influence a student's academic success. Undocumented students, many of whom are SLIFE, experience significant difficulties, such as completing graduation requirements, resisting pressure to drop out in favor of paid work, and pursuing seemingly unattainable higher education prospects. According to Zong and Batalova (2019), only about 98,000 undocumented students graduate from U.S. high schools annually. However, a staggering 40 percent of undocumented adolescents drop out of high school, compared to only 8 percent of their U.S.-born peers (Perez, 2014, as cited in Manspile et al., 2021). Perez (2014) identifies financial burdens, the fear of revealing one's legal status, and a lack of support toward attaining postsecondary education as three major contributors.

Many SLIFE, particularly those who are refugees, are also afflicted by stress related to trauma, acculturation, isolation, and resettlement

(Boston Children's Hospital, 2019). These students often have trouble fitting in at school and forming a new multicultural identity.

Age, too, can play a significant role in the language and content acquisition process for all MLs. In the case of SLIFE at the secondary level, age is an important factor in determining placement. This can result in such suboptimal scenarios as a 16-year-old with a 3rd-grade skill level being enrolled in 9th grade. The discrepancy between a student's age and their actual skill level can certainly leave educators feeling perplexed since many of the resources that their students actually need, based on their skill level, are significantly below the grade-appropriate resources that they are expected to implement.

MLs with Disabilities

MLs with disabilities are a growing and underserved subpopulation of MLs (Fagan & Herrera, 2022). These are students who are eligible for both special education services and multilingual learner services. According to Fagan and Herrera (2022), "English learners with disabilities accounted for 9.5 percent of all students with individualized education programs (IEPs) in 2013–14 and 11.28 percent in 2019–20 (about 830,000 students)" (p. 2). A full 93 percent of these students receive IEPs for a specific learning disability, speech/language impairment, or intellectual disability; the rest receive special education services for low-incidence disabilities such as hearing or visual impairment or traumatic brain injury (Fagan & Herrera, 2022).

Although disability categories can vary from state to state, federal law ensures that MLs must be evaluated in both English and their native language in order to ensure the disability is separate from challenges stemming from the language acquisition process. Nevertheless, concerns over the accuracy of the identification process continue. MLs receiving special education services, and those in need of such services, have unique academic and social-emotional needs that require educators with specific training and expertise. Watkins and Liu (2013) note that serving this population of students requires specialized staff recruitment and training as well as materials and assessments in the home languages of the MLs and their families.

Long-Term English Learners

Another group of struggling MLs includes long-term English learners (LTELs). According to Freeman and Freeman (2002), SLIFE and LTELs are the two groups of MLs that "experience the most difficulty in school" (p. 5). LTELs are often found in grades 6–12 and are defined as having spent seven or more years in the United States. They typically have adequate grades but score poorly on standardized tests and are at risk of dropping out. They have limited literacy in both their home language and English and have experienced inconsistent English language development (ELD) instruction (Freeman & Freeman, 2002; Menken & Kleyn, 2009; Olsen & Jaramillo, 1999). A strength of LTELs is their tendency to have strong oral skills in both English and their native language; however, they struggle when it comes to academic literacy skills (Cashiola & Potter, 2020; Olsen, 2014).

The Unique Strengths of MLs

Despite the very real challenges faced by SLIFE and other struggling MLs, we know that these students also bring many strengths to our classrooms and communities. Many of them are newcomers who bring rich experiences, customs, and backgrounds that can help them adapt and thrive in a new community (Massachusetts Department of Elementary and Secondary Education, 2022a). González and colleagues (2005) refer to these strengths as funds of knowledge, which include their home language, cultural knowledge, artifacts, and resources. Their global perspective, extensive pragmatic knowledge and skills, and rich cultural backgrounds are strengths that our SLIFE possess and that can be drawn upon for achieving academic success (Massachusetts Department of Elementary and Secondary Education, 2022b). Therefore, effective, equitable instruction of these students must incorporate culturally responsive instruction that supports academic achievement, literacy, and social-emotional learning (SEL).

Research, however, does not seem to do justice to the strengths that our MLs show us on a daily basis. The MLs with whom we've worked have shown us what it means to create an unparalleled sense of community in a classroom. For example, after just three weeks in class, Allen asked us if he could bring in a cake to celebrate his birthday with his classmates. It was only after we had enjoyed the delicious cake and were cleaning up that Allen told us this was his first time having classmates and going to school.

More often than not, MLs are quick to form connections and help their peers with tasks, even when there are risks involved. For example, despite having been told not to talk or collaborate during a quiz, our student Manuel proceeded to help a friend who had recently enrolled in the class. When we brought this up with him, his response was "But Miss, he doesn't understand"—showing that he placed his desire to help his new friend above the risk of failing his quiz. Manuel's empathetic response was a testament to the struggles he had experienced firsthand as an ML himself.

Two other students, Kiara and Julio, started in our self-contained SLIFE classes, but their unwavering determination helped them quickly move through the levels and, ultimately, enroll in college. These two students had every reason not to complete their homework each night— they went directly from school to their jobs, one at a factory and the other at a restaurant, until the early-morning hours. Despite facing far greater pressures and responsibilities than most teenagers their age, they never gave up on their academic goals. Kiara was even able to participate in the school's newly formed early college program, which enabled her to take courses at a local community college while still enrolled in high school. And showing that there is absolutely no limit to what a SLIFE can do, Julio was one of our co-presenters at an education conference.

Obstacles Faced by Educators of SLIFE and Other Struggling MLs

Challenges, however, are not unique to SLIFE and other struggling MLs. Educators of these students encounter their own set of obstacles—obstacles that include a lack of effective strategies and scaffolds, a shortage of adequate curricular resources, and, very importantly, a focus on standardized testing.

Research shows that the strategies teachers use in the classroom have a significant impact on student literacy skills (Cohan & Honigsfeld, 2017; Li & Zhang, 2004; Menken, 2013; Montero et al., 2014; Windle & Miller, 2012). Unfortunately, Li and Zhang (2004) found that many teachers working with SLIFE are not aware of strategies that can help them meet their students' needs. In the case of teachers working with SLIFE at the secondary level, Windle and Miller (2012) noted the unpopularity of text-based supports for scaffolding and hypothesized that this may be due to the scarcity of appropriate resources and the time constraints that prevent them from creating such resources from scratch.

Time constraints affect all educators of SLIFE and struggling MLs. As teachers try to navigate the challenges of aligning instruction to grade-level standards, they find themselves confined to implementing resources that are often well above their students' skill levels. However, the alternative of providing resources aligned to students' skill levels is equally problematic as these resources are designed for much younger learners and do not offer the level of complexity, rigor, and age-appropriate context that students will encounter in mainstream classes, let alone on standardized assessments. Some educators choose to create their own resources—but how does one even begin to create an ELA text for a 20-year-old who only completed 2nd grade in his native country? Doing this takes time—a *lot* of time. To further complicate matters, teachers are pressured to follow a prescribed scope and sequence that does not leave much room for the extra time and support that SLIFE need.

As the emphasis on standardized testing increases in U.S. schools, so does the pressure that educators and students alike face. Citing Creagh (2019) and Giouroukakis and Honigsfeld (2010), Filimon (2023) shows that SLIFE are not exempt from standardized testing requirements and are expected to participate in grade-level content-area tests, similar to their mainstream peers. Consequently, educators feel compelled to emphasize preparing students to meet the demands of such high-stakes assessments, as Creagh (2019) notes. Such emphasis, DeCapua and Marshall (2011a, 2015) underscore, forces teachers to devote extensive time to test preparation activities, preventing them from appropriately addressing the needs of their learners.

In the face of so many seemingly insurmountable challenges, it comes as no surprise that educators of SLIFE and other struggling MLs often feel defeated before they even begin to figure out how to address the needs of their students. As educators, we totally get it. We want the best for our students but don't always know what "the best" looks like in the classroom on a daily basis. The following chapters provide you with practical strategies you can use with your students. It is our hope that this book will empower all educators of SLIFE and struggling MLs to swap that mismatched elementary-style curricular resource for your teenaged SLIFE with an age-appropriate, relevant adapted text and scaffolds designed to address their literacy needs. We hope you will engage your secondary-level SLIFE with standards-based, rigorous instruction that can help prepare them to meet graduation requirements. It's our wish that you will be empowered to involve your exhausted wage earner in interactive, student-centered learning activities that integrate all four language domains.

How This Book Is Organized

As you explore this book, you will see that we have organized our strategies and instructional resources by language domain.

In Chapter 1, you will learn about practical resources and templates for engaging SLIFE and struggling MLs in academic conversation, thus targeting the speaking and listening domains. Many SLIFE and struggling MLs have strong oral language skills in their native language (Alvarez, 2020; Barba et al., 2019; DeCapua, 2016; DeCapua & Marshall, 2011a, 2015; Digby, 2019; Hos et al., 2019; Kennedy & Lamina, 2016). Chapter 1 focuses on ways to develop this strength to help students learn academic English.

Chapter 2 is dedicated to equipping educators with strategies for developing the reading skills of SLIFE and other struggling MLs. This chapter focuses on proven reading comprehension strategies specifically designed to help SLIFE and other struggling MLs interact with texts in all phases of the reading process.

The focus of Chapter 3 is on enabling students to achieve success in academic writing. This chapter provides an overview of our highly successful, research-based writing protocol adapted specifically for SLIFE and other struggling MLs. Using colors to represent the key elements of a written response, this protocol allows students to identify the patterns in academic writing.

In Chapter 4, we discuss our spiraling approach to instruction, designed to meet the needs of SLIFE and other struggling MLs at the forefront. Now equipped with a toolbox of strategies presented in Chapters 1 through 3, readers learn how to maximize their effectiveness by rethinking traditional approaches to instruction. Based on Bruner's (1960) concept of spiral curriculum, our model focuses on revisiting key language skills multiple times throughout the year—a significant departure from traditional instructional approaches, which progress in a linear manner from basic to more complex skills. We have found the spiraling model to be highly effective with SLIFE and other struggling MLs. All students have opportunities to either learn or go deeper, thus simultaneously advancing their English learning and content knowledge.

The final chapter provides a complete unit aligned to the Common Core State Standards and is broken down into daily lessons that put into practice the strategies outlined in the preceding chapters. This unit is inspired by the Understanding by Design framework (Wiggins & McTighe, 2005) and the principles of project-based learning (PBL). Each lesson includes a language and content objective, SEL connections, an agenda of activities and assessments, and reproducible resources. The unit focuses on an engaging and relevant topic—the impacts of technology—and culminates in a class debate.

Five Guiding Principles

You will find five guiding principles throughout this book that are drawn from our own experience and that we believe will enhance your instruction and foster learning:

1. **Take a spiraling approach.** MLs (and learners in general) need concepts to be revisited and reinforced. Instead of following a linear approach that builds on increasingly complex language, concepts, and skills, take time to revisit concepts systematically and explicitly. You will find that this approach enables you to reach more students. New students will have an opportunity to learn concepts at any point in the school year, struggling students will have a second (and third and fourth) chance to learn, and advanced students will be able to deepen their understanding. We encourage you to spiral all language skills, including those related to grammar and pronunciation.

2. **Make time to talk.** It is important to make time for peer-to-peer interactions among students. Many of the strategies in this book focus on ways to increase student talk time. As the saying goes, the person speaking most is learning most—and that is especially true for SLIFE and struggling MLs.

3. **Be consistent.** You will see that many of the same sentence stems are used across various activities and scaffolds in this book. Keeping the sentence stems consistent ensures that struggling MLs internalize them and can use them effectively once the scaffolds are removed. Consistency also reduces the cognitive load associated with learning new information and builds confidence in students.

4. **Remember that there is no *L* without *SEL*.** Many of the strategies in this book are designed to connect MLs with one another so they can reflect on their lives, their communities, and society at large while collaborating to meet academic goals. We strongly believe that integrating SEL into instruction isn't just another box to check; rather, social-emotional learning *is* the box. In learning past-tense verbs, students develop the SEL competency of communication; when they give a presentation, they build their self-confidence; as they research a problem and brainstorm solutions, they are problem solving, analyzing situations, and evaluating. We encourage you to display and go over the SEL competencies that you are addressing every day along with your language and content objectives.

   Students, especially MLs, learn best when their learning is connected to their social and emotional needs. Establishing a safe learning environment is paramount to the second-language acquisition process. Some academic topics can seem abstract to many SLIFE, so connecting them explicitly to students' lives can increase motivation and make learning more meaningful and engaging.

5. **Raise the bar.** Remember that you are dealing with uncommon learners who have a history of overcoming challenges. Allow yourself to take instructional risks and you will see your students soar to new academic heights. Keep your expectations high and help students meet them by designing appropriate scaffolds rather than lowering the bar by watering down the curriculum. As we know from experience, when teachers and students take risks, learning is *unlimited*.

We are thrilled to share this book with you in hopes that you will be able to implement the strategies in your own classroom with your own students, as we have. If you do, we'd love to hear your experiences and feedback. Above all, we hope that the contents of this book enable you to foster the unlimited potential of your students.

Now It's Your Turn: Questions and Exercises

- Describe your students. Do their struggles mirror any of the struggles discussed in this chapter?
- Reflect on your students' strengths. What assets do they bring to the classroom? Do their strengths mirror any of the strengths discussed in this chapter?
- What strategies are you currently implementing in your teaching? What have you found to be most successful with your SLIFE and/or struggling MLs?

1

Speak Up: Strategies for Supporting Academic Conversations

Educators of SLIFE and other struggling MLs are often cognizant of the many obstacles their students face in U.S. schools. However, they must also recognize the strengths that these learners bring to their classrooms and leverage those strengths to help them learn. Many of these students, especially SLIFE, come from cultures with a strong emphasis on oral language as the primary medium for sharing information and connecting with others (DeCapua & Marshall, 2010, 2011b). In this chapter, you will learn about effective strategies and resources specifically designed to engage SLIFE and other struggling MLs in academic conversation. You will find a wide variety of sentence stems for higher-order thinking skills, such as comparing and contrasting, expressing an opinion, and citing textual evidence—which are at the heart of our instructional protocols. You will also find multiple versatile tools that can be easily adapted to fit the context of your classroom, such as turn-and-talk templates, presentation tents, note-taking templates, and debate scaffolds (among others).

Although mainstream students and MLs struggle at times with the demands of academic conversation, adolescent SLIFE and newcomer MLs face even greater obstacles due to their limited language skills and lack of familiarity with the written and unwritten rules of school-based discourse. Academic dialogue challenges students to advance their thinking, yet rich and purposeful conversation is too often inconsistently threaded through mainstream instruction (Zwiers & Crawford, 2011). It's no surprise that MLs have difficulty explaining their reasoning, especially in areas such as math and science, which require extensive knowledge of specific vocabulary and expressions. In addition, such content areas pose greater difficulty to SLIFE and other struggling MLs in terms of mastering the grammatical structures involved in writing a scientific report, explaining the order of operations, and adapting their speech to fit the goals of the task (Rose, 2017; Schleppegrell, 2001). To further complicate matters, the Common Core State Standards (CCSS) for math and science assume that students have already gained a solid foundation in those subjects by the time they enter high school (Wright, 2015). As Fenner (2013) notes, "The CCSS stresses that all students—including ELs—must master academic language so that they can successfully perform such CCSS-required tasks as persuading, citing evidence, and engaging with complex informational texts" (p. 7).

Though oral language growth is critical for developing literacy (Wright, 2015) and has become a critical shift in the CCSS (Zwiers & Crawford, 2011), academic conversations, presentations, debates, and Socratic seminars are rarely used with SLIFE and newcomer MLs. Misconceptions surrounding the belief that MLs, especially SLIFE, must first develop basic English language and vocabulary skills to engage in academic conversations is one possible explanation. Furthermore, although it can be tempting for teachers to speak the most when their learners are not fully proficient in English, it is precisely this category of learners that need the most opportunities to practice academic discourse (Echevarría et al., 2004). In addition, many educators approach higher-order thinking skills progressively with MLs, focusing first on remembering and comprehending and only later on skills such as evaluating and analyzing. Some educators still believe that students in the early stages of learning English literacy should focus exclusively on reading and writing tasks.

Silence, in general, is not perceived as a mark of a highly engaging and interactive language-learning environment. However, silence is often the outcome in classrooms in which MLs struggle with how to express themselves authentically in their new language. Prior to developing our model, we'd ask our students to turn and talk and hear . . . nothing. We would try rephrasing the question . . . silence. We would point to generic sentence stems we had displayed on the wall to provide linguistic support . . . still nothing. At most, students would converse in their native language. But turning and talking about the topic at hand in English was rare.

Engaging students in presentations came with its own set of struggles. Some of these struggles stem from the fact that, as teachers, we are accustomed to focusing on the presenter rather than the audience during an oral presentation. As one of the writers of this book experienced firsthand, we once received feedback from an evaluator who said that one student—the presenter—looked very engaged while presenting his work. "But what are all the other students doing?" the evaluator asked. This question led the teacher to turn what had been a passive listening activity for the audience into a meaningful academic exchange.

Our experiences inspired us to design interactive templates for a range of speaking and listening activities. As you will see in this chapter, we have added scaffolds to traditional turn-and-talk and presentation strategies that have made a world of difference in our classrooms.

Academic Sentence Stems

The effectiveness of sentence stems as a linguistic support for students cannot be overstated (e.g., Cotterall & Cohen, 2003; Gottlieb, 2016; Kim et al., 2011; Olson et al., 2012, 2015, 2017; Windle & Miller, 2019). In this section, we share a set of sentence stems designed to support higher-order thinking skills created specifically for MLs at the lowest level of English proficiency and literacy. These sentence stems have proven to be more than simply scaffolding tools; they are central to our approach of fostering academic language development across all four language domains and serve as a foundation for many of the strategies you will find throughout this book.

The Challenge

The CCSS hold all students accountable for mastering academic language, including MLs (Fenner, 2013). Teachers have tried to address these issues by using generic sets of sentence stems; however, these sets are typically intended for students with a greater level of English proficiency than that of entering MLs and SLIFE. On the other hand, the level of rigor of the few resources available for these students falls short of meeting the demands of the CCSS.

Our Approach

We were inspired to adapt existing sentence stems as well as to develop our own by Kinsella's work creating frames for accountable talk (Dutro & Kinsella, 2010; Kinsella, 2005; Kinsella & Feldman, 2005). Drawing on this framework of selecting higher-order thinking concepts, such as asking for clarification, agreeing and disagreeing, and expressing an opinion, we developed a comprehensive series of sentence stems specifically tailored for entering MLs and SLIFE, thus fast-tracking their ability to understand and produce academic discourse. In our work with SLIFE and other struggling MLs, we have come to find that less is more. In other words, we have found greater success employing the same sentence stems more often instead of constantly introducing new ones. We typically use the same three to five stems for each skill. When introducing the stems, we usually begin with just one or two and add more each time we revisit the skill over the school year. Using the same sentence stems allows for greater consistency and automaticity, resulting in a faster rate of language acquisition.

Figure 1.1 shows the sentence stems we recommend according to the skills they help students develop. The first column shows the sentence stems we adapted from the work of Kinsella (2005) to fit the needs of

FIGURE 1.1

Academic Sentence Stems

Adapted Stems	Additional Stems
Asking for Clarification	**Making an Observation**
• I have a question about _____. • Excuse me, can you please repeat _____? • Can you clarify what you said about _____?	• I can see _____. • I observe _____. • I notice _____.
Justifying an Opinion	**Making an Inference**
• I think _____ because _____. • I believe _____ because _____. • In my opinion, _____. • From my perspective, _____. • From my point of view, _____. • My reasons are _____.	• I can infer _____ because _____. • Based on the picture/the text/my experience, I can infer _____.
Reporting a Partner's Idea	**Citing Textual Evidence**
• _____ said that _____. • _____ explained to me that _____. • According to _____, _____.	• The text says _____. • According to the text, _____. • Based on the text, _____. • The author explains that _____.
Offering a Suggestion	**Sequencing**
• I suggest _____. • I recommend _____. • My suggestion is _____. • My recommendation is _____.	• First, _____. • Second, _____. • After, _____. • Then, _____. • Next, _____. • Finally, _____.
Agreeing	**Comparing and Contrasting**
• I agree with _____ because _____. • I share your opinion because _____. • My perspective is similar to _____'s because _____.	• _____ is similar to _____ because _____. • _____ is different from _____ because _____. • The similarities are _____. • The differences are _____.
Disagreeing	**Cause and Effect**
• I disagree with _____ because _____. • I don't share your opinion because _____. • My perspective is different from _____'s because _____. • You said _____. However, I think _____.	• _____ because _____. • _____. As a result, _____. • _____. Therefore, _____. • _____ since _____.

(continued)

FIGURE 1.1—*(continued)*
Academic Sentence Stems

Adapted Stems	Additional Stems
	Adding Information • Also, _____. • In addition, _____. • Additionally, _____. • Furthermore, _____. • For example, _____.
	Evaluating Information • The advantages are _____. • The disadvantages are _____. • _____ is better because _____. • The best option is _____ because _____.

Note: The stems in the first column are based on Kinsella (2005). Adapted with permission.

SLIFE and other struggling MLs, whereas the second column shows the additional sentence stems we developed ourselves.

Turn-and-Talk Template

The Why

We developed our turn-and-talk template (Figure 1.2) to maximize speaking during routine activities and to clarify for students what to ask and how to respond using academic language. This sample template allows for higher student engagement and student-to-student interaction by eliminating the teacher question–student response cycle. Because the questions and sentence stems are created in advance, they can be especially deliberate and strategic. This strategy also allows for differentiation in mixed-level classrooms since the sentence stems can be easily changed or removed.

The What

Perhaps the greatest advantage of this tool is its simplicity in design and use. This template consists of one column for Student A and one for Student B. In the Student A column are rows with questions for the "turn-and-talk" discussion. In the Student B column are rows with sentence stems that help students know how to start their response.

FIGURE 1.2

Turn-and-Talk Template

Student A (Question)	Student B (Response)
1. What are some ways you use technology at home?	Some ways I use technology at home are _____.
2. What are some ways you use technology at school?	Some ways I use technology at school are _____.
3. How does technology have a positive impact on your life?	Technology has a positive impact because _____.
4. How does technology have a negative impact on your life?	Technology has a negative impact because _____.
5. Is technology making our lives better or worse?	In my opinion, technology is making our lives _____ because _____.

The How

This tool can be used any time your goal is to have students interact with one another. It can also be used to assess students' background knowledge, reinforce academic sentence stems, and/or build fluency. It can be used in conjunction with a text, video, or picture or in any situation in which you want students to engage in academic discussion. When implementing this strategy in your ELD or content-area classes, use or create questions that match the objectives of your lesson. Then think about how you would respond to the same questions. What language would indicate a well-crafted response? The answers you come up with can serve as the sentence stems in column B. Before asking students to turn and talk, model the use of this template by taking on the role of Student A and asking one or two questions to a student volunteer. Then switch roles. When students are ready, they will take turns turning and talking with a peer.

Materials

- Turn-and-talk template

Presentations

The Why

Although mainstream students and MLs alike struggle with giving formal academic presentations, adolescent SLIFE and newcomer MLs often face additional challenges due to limited language skills and unfamiliarity with the format and structure of formal presentations. Yet even after such challenges are addressed, engaging students in presentations can still be a struggle.

With the stakes as high as they are for our MLs, students cannot afford any missed speaking or active listening opportunities. Although the act of giving a presentation is cognitively demanding for the presenters, it is often a missed opportunity for the rest of the class to participate. In many instances, the audience is tasked with asking generic questions, such as "What was your favorite/least favorite part of this project?" or "If you were to give this presentation again, what would you do differently?"

There is a time and place for such questions, but active listening and engaging with the presenter provides a more enriching learning experience—one in which the audience must listen, comprehend, and demonstrate their understanding of what they heard. There is also an opportunity to ask clarification and elaboration questions. Familiarity with such exchanges empowers students to ask questions in many situations, both inside and outside the classroom, when they do not understand what they hear. With that in mind, we've developed a suite of presentation tools.

The How

When students have finished creating a PowerPoint or Google Slides presentation, prepare them for their upcoming presentations by modeling the use of the template. If desired, the frames could be cut and put on index cards for students to use during their presentations. Be sure students have adequate time to practice and prepare for their presentation. In addition, you will want to explain the rubric to students ahead of time so expectations will be clear and they will be aware of how their performance will be assessed. When it's showtime, pass out the interactive note-taking template that students will use to take notes on their peers' presentations. Circulate as they complete it during the first presentation. If students leave any spaces blank, assist them in asking the clarification and elaboration questions to the presenter. Continue to assist students as they jot down notes during this phase. As the presentations continue, you will find that students will be able to interact with the presenter with little assistance from you.

Materials

- **Presentation frames template** and **sample presentation frames template** (Figures 1.3 and 1.4): The presentation frames are sentence frames we developed to allow students to introduce themselves, transition between ideas, and conclude their presentations.
- **Interactive note-taking template** (Figures 1.5 and 1.6): This template is geared toward audience members, enabling them to listen and take notes as well as ask clarification and elaboration questions when the presentation concludes. The questions on the template include "Excuse me, can you please repeat what you said about _____?" "Excuse me, can you please clarify _____?" and "That was interesting. Can you please tell me more about _____?" The blanks correspond to the information in the table (e.g., "Excuse me, can you please repeat what you said about the advantages?" or "That was interesting. Can you please tell me more about the disadvantages?").

This sample template could be used in an ELD class in conjunction with presentations on the pros and cons of technology, or the top row of the template could be modified to fit the context of a different presentation. To give you an opportunity to see what this tool looks like in action, we have included a completed template. This student sample should give you a sense of what it would look like to have students engage in this sort of activity in one of your classes. As you can see from the example—which is from a self-contained biology course designed for SLIFE at the secondary level—this template can be adapted and used in any content area in which students are giving a presentation. In this particular instance, students had to fill out the interactive note-taking template as they watched their peers deliver food web presentations. We typically collect and use this template as a formative or summative assessment tool to check listening comprehension.

- **Table tent for elaboration and clarification** (Figure 1.7): In addition to providing sentence stems to students as part of a handout, we have found increased effectiveness by placing them on students' desks as a "table tent" for easy access. This tent can be adapted to fit a range of presentation types, but we typically use it when students are delivering a PowerPoint or Google Slides presentation.

- **Presentation rubric** (Figure 1.8): The presentation rubric is written in student-friendly language using "I can" statements and can be used as a formative or summative assessment tool. The rubric is designed to be completed by teachers. An example of a completed rubric with feedback is provided.

FIGURE 1.3

Presentation Frames Template

Introduction	Good [morning/afternoon]. My name is _____. Today, I will present about _____. I hope you enjoy my presentation.
Main Content	First, I will explain about _____. (Explain in your words.)
	Next, I will explain about _____. (Explain in your words.)
	Additionally, I will explain about _____. (Explain in your words.)
	Finally, I will explain about _____. (Explain in your words.)
Conclusion	This concludes my presentation. Thank you for listening. Do you have any questions?

FIGURE 1.4

Sample Presentation Frames Template

Note: This example shows a frame adapted for a presentation in which students are asked to explain the advantages and disadvantages of various technological items in their lives.

Introduction	Good morning/afternoon. My name is _____. Today, I will present about how _____ impacts our lives. I hope you enjoy my presentation.
Main Content	First, I will explain how _____ impacts our daily lives. (Explain in your words.)
	Now, I will explain the advantages of _____. (Explain in your words.)
	Also, I will explain the disadvantages of _____. (Explain in your words.)
	In my opinion, _____. (Explain in your words.)
Conclusion	This concludes my presentation. Thank you for listening. Do you have any questions?

FIGURE 1.5

Interactive Note-Taking Template

Name: _____   Date: _____

Excuse me, can you please repeat what you said about _____?

Excuse me, can you please clarify _____?

That was interesting. Can you please tell me more about _____?

Presenter	Technological Device	Advantages	Disadvantages

FIGURE 1.6

Sample Interactive Note-Taking Template

Name: Gabriel Marquis   **Date:** March 11, 2025

Excuse me, can you please repeat what you said about _____?

Excuse me, can you please clarify _____?

That was interesting. Can you please tell me more about _____?

Presenter	Producers	Primary Consumers	Secondary Consumers	Tertiary Consumers	Decomposers
Reinaldo	Flower Berries	Mouse Grasshopper Squirrel Rabbit	Fox Frog Snake Mouse	Owl	Mushroom
Eliseo	Flower Berries Grass	Mouse Rabbit Deer	Snake Coyote	Hawk Puma	Mushroom

Note: This sample is from a self-contained science class for SLIFE students.

FIGURE 1.7

Table Tent for Elaboration and Clarification

Excuse me, can you please repeat the _____ ?

Excuse me, can you clarify what you said about _____ ?

That was interesting. Can you please tell me more about _____ ?

FIGURE 1.8

Presentation Rubric

Criteria	Level 1	Level 2	Level 3
Pronunciation	I have **many** pronunciation errors.	I have **some** pronunciation errors.	I have **few** pronunciation errors.
Completeness	My presentation is **incomplete.**	My presentation is **mostly complete.**	My presentation is **complete** and demonstrates effort.
Paraphrasing	I **read** from slides. I do not look at the audience.	I **sometimes** read from slides. I sometimes look at the audience.	I **do not** read from slides. I always look at the audience. I paraphrase and explain ideas in my own words.
Vocabulary	I can use **simple** social and academic vocabulary.	I use **general and some content-specific** academic vocabulary.	I use **general and many content-specific** academic vocabulary.
Knowledgeability	I **cannot** answer questions from the audience about my presentation.	I can answer **some** questions from the audience about my presentation.	I can answer **many** questions from the audience about my presentation and can give additional details.
Grammar	Grammatical errors make my message **unclear.**	Grammatical errors make my message **somewhat unclear.**	Grammatical errors do not interfere with my message. My message is **clear.**

Debates

The Why

Academic debates provide opportunities for students to express their opinions, cite textual evidence, and apply what they have read. Students, especially MLs, develop fluency through the rapid exchange of ideas as well as social-emotional learning competencies, such as respecting others, evaluating, reflecting, analyzing situations, and monitoring impulse control (CASEL, 2020). Despite these benefits, however, it is extremely rare to see MLs at the lowest level of English proficiency engaging in debates.

We believe this is due in part to the scarcity of data on the topic and age-appropriate resources that address the needs of these students.

Like many teachers, we were reluctant to have our SLIFE and struggling MLs engage in debate. Nevertheless, we wanted to give it a try. For our students to succeed, we knew they needed to be knowledgeable about the topic they were debating and, importantly, personally invested in it. Our first debate topic was a source of tension with which many teachers are familiar: school uniforms. This casual, but often passionate, exchange was actually the fuel for our first-ever academic debate. We had students make a list of pros and cons, practice using transition words such as *also* and *however*, and sort arguments and counterarguments. When it came time for them to debate, students performed so impressively that we decided to incorporate frequent opportunities for debate into our teaching practice. In the process, we developed the following debate scaffolds and resources.

The What

The following materials have proven to be effective for engaging SLIFE and other struggling MLs in rigorous academic debate. We would like to emphasize that these resources have proven to be effective with MLs at various proficiency levels, including newcomer SLIFE.

The How

As students gained familiarity with the structure and routines of debates, we expanded the topics to include a range of disciplines and contexts. For SLIFE and entering MLs, those at the lowest level of English proficiency, we found that debate works best as a culminating project. In other words, students have already prepared for extended academic discourse by first using the vocabulary and reading strategies shared throughout this book. With these preparations in place, students have had time to build background knowledge, read and analyze texts, and speak and write extensively about the topic. Now they are ready for the next step. To prepare students for debate, we start by giving an overview of the debate structure and chunking the debate and debate preparation into several parts.

The debate consists of three parts: the opening statements (by both pro and con teams), the rebuttal phase, and closing statements (by both teams)—a classroom application of this strategy is explained in detail in Chapter 5. We start by dividing students into two teams. Each team uses the T-notes graphic organizer to list arguments and counterarguments for and against their position. We have found success using red and green colored pencils to emphasize opposing ideas. Then, using only the arguments that support their claims, each team drafts an opening statement. At this point, they also decide who is going to read which part; typically, students read between one and three sentences each during the opening statements. Each team can also create visuals to accompany their opening statements, which can help scaffold understanding if pronunciation errors impede comprehension.

During the rebuttal phase of the debate, students disagree with the opposing team's ideas using sentence stems on table tents. As students become familiar with these sentence stems, additional stems and transition words can be added, such as *on the other hand* and *although*. The table tents allow for a gradual reduction in scaffolding. Unlike the opening statements, students do not prepare notes for the rebuttal in advance; they must first listen to the arguments before expressing their ideas. However, they are not without support. They can use the table tent to know exactly how to start and form their response.

For the closing statement, students can use sentence stems on table tents. In this last phase, they must sum up their own arguments rather than rebut those of the other team. As students progress in their language acquisition, this phase of the debate can also come to include rhetorical questions and the language of persuasion.

During all three sections of the debate, every student is expected to speak at least once. The only phase of the debate that is extensively scaffolded is the opening statement; the rebuttal and closing statements should be created on the spot to develop fluency. We recommend practicing the debate two or three times to build confidence, establish familiarity with the structure and expectations, and hone pronunciation skills.

While the teacher scores students using the debate rubric, a judge (usually a colleague) can be invited in to score students, often adding an extra layer of engagement. Judges use the debate scoring template to take notes during the debate, score the performance of each team, and share their feedback. We have had administrators, guidance counselors, and other teachers act as honorary judges in the past. We'd like to emphasize that although the scoring template is used to evaluate each team's performance, the debate rubric is used for evaluating the performance of individual students.

Materials

- **T-notes graphic organizer** (Figures 1.9 and 1.10): This chart is for listing arguments and counterarguments.
- **Opening statement graphic organizer** (Figure 1.11): This chart has sentence frames for constructing an opening statement.
- **Rebuttal table tent** (Figure 1.12): This table tent includes sentence stems to help students articulate counterarguments.
- **Closing statement table tent** (Figure 1.13): This table tent includes sentence stems to help students conclude their portion of the debate.
- **Debate scoring template** (Figure 1.14): This form is for the judge to use when judging debate performances (optional). We have also included a sample completed template used to assess team performance in a debate on the merits of oil drilling (Figure 1.15).
- **Debate rubric** (Figure 1.16): This is the rubric—outlining success criteria—to use for determining debate scores.

FIGURE 1.9

T-Notes Graphic Organizer

Technology: Advantages and Disadvantages

Complete the organizer by listing the advantages and disadvantages of using technology. Remember to use examples from the text we read in class as well as brainstorm your own examples.

Advantages	Disadvantages
1.	1.
2.	2.
3.	3.
4.	4.
5.	5.

FIGURE 1.10

Sample T-Notes Graphic Organizer

Technology: Advantages and Disadvantages

Complete the organizer by listing the advantages and disadvantages of using technology. Remember to use examples from the text we read in class as well as brainstorm your own examples.

Advantages	Disadvantages
1. Technology helps us do activities faster.	1. Technology can be distracting for students.
2. We can use technology to communicate.	2. Using cell phones when driving is distracting and dangerous.
3. People can use technology for transportation.	3. People spend a lot of time on social media and apps.
4. We can find information and learn new things.	4. Walking and riding bikes is better for our health and the environment than cars and buses.
5. Doctors can use technology in hospitals to save people's lives.	5. When we use technology like calculators and GPS, we use our minds less.

FIGURE 1.11

Opening Statement Graphic Organizer

Name: _____   **Date:** _____   **Class:** _____

Student Name(s)	Opening Statement
	Our team believes that technology is making our lives _____ for a variety of reasons.
	First of all, we believe that _____. According to the text, _____ _____.
	Also, we think that _____. Based on the text, _____ _____.
	In addition, we believe that _____. The text says, _____ _____.
	As you can see, technology is _____ for many reasons: _____, _____, and _____.

FIGURE 1.12
Rebuttal Table Tent

I disagree with what you said about _____

However, I believe _____

FIGURE 1.13
Closing Statement Table Tent

As you can see, _____

To sum up, _____

FIGURE 1.14

Debate Scoring Template

1 = approaches   2 = meets   3 = exceeds

Part 1: Opening Statements	Group 1 (PRO)	Group 2 (CON)
All students speak.	1 2 3	1 2 3
Students support reasons with details and textual evidence.	1 2 3	1 2 3
Students use transition words (e.g., *first, next, also*).	1 2 3	1 2 3
Pronunciation is clear.	1 2 3	1 2 3
Total:		

Notes:

Part 2: Rebuttal	Group 1 (PRO)	Group 2 (CON)
All students speak.	1 2 3	1 2 3
Students argue against specific claims made by the opposing team.	1 2 3	1 2 3
Students use transition words (e.g., *however, on the other hand*).	1 2 3	1 2 3
Pronunciation is clear.	1 2 3	1 2 3
Students consult notes but do NOT read them.	1 2 3	1 2 3
Total:		

Notes:

Part 3: Closing Statements	Group 1 (PRO)	Group 2 (CON)
All students speak.	1 2 3	1 2 3
Students use transition words (e.g., *in conclusion, all in all, to sum up*).	1 2 3	1 2 3
Pronunciation is clear.	1 2 3	1 2 3
Students summarize their ideas and do not argue or restate their opening statements.	1 2 3	1 2 3
Total:		

Notes:

GRAND TOTAL:	

FIGURE 1.15
Sample Debate Scoring Template

1 = approaches   2 = meets   3 = exceeds

Part 1: Opening Statements	Group 1 (PRO)	Group 2 (CON)
All students speak.	1 2 (3)	1 2 (3)
Students support reasons with details and textual evidence.	1 (2) 3	1 2 (3)
Students use transition words (e.g., *first, next, also*).	1 2 (3)	1 2 (3)
Pronunciation is clear.	1 (2) 3	1 (2) 3
Total:	(10)	(11)

Notes: Group 1 key points: oil drilling benefits the economy; oil drilling creates jobs, "energy independence"
**Needs text evidence

Group 2 key points: oil drilling harms animals, ecosystems; oil spills cost millions of dollars to clean; we can use "renewable energy"

(continued)

FIGURE 1.15—(*continued*)
Sample Debate Scoring Template

1 = approaches   2 = meets   3 = exceeds

Part 2: Rebuttal	Group 1 (PRO)	Group 2 (CON)
All students speak.	1 ②3	1 2 ③
Students argue against specific claims made by the opposing team.	1 2 ③	1 ②3
Students use transition words (e.g., *however, on the other hand*).	1 2 ③	1 2 ③
Pronunciation is clear.	1 ②3	1 ②3
Students consult notes but do NOT read them.	1 2 ③	1 ②3
Total:	⑬	⑫

Notes: Group 1: Maria and Franklyn did not participate; students used table tents but didn't read!

Group 2: All students participated, but some relied on notes and reread parts of the opening statement; some parts felt disjointed as some students did not clearly connect counterclaims to specific claims by the other team.

Part 3: Closing Statements	Group 1 (PRO)	Group 2 (CON)
All students speak.	1 2 ③	1 2 ③
Students use transition words (e.g., *in conclusion, all in all, to sum up*).	1 2 ③	1 2 ③
Pronunciation is clear.	1 ②3	1 ②3
Students summarize their ideas and do not argue or restate their opening statements.	1 2 ③	1 ②3
Total:	⑪	⑩

Notes: All students spoke – Group 1 was stronger at providing conclusions, whereas Group 2 seemed to continue the rebuttal phase.

GRAND TOTAL:	㉞	㉝

Notes: Both teams did a great job! But team 1 had a stronger rebuttal (they more clearly connected their arguments and counterclaims) and a stronger conclusion.

FIGURE 1.16

Debate Rubric

Criteria	Approaching 1	Good 2	Excellent 3
Pronunciation (Opening Statement)	I have **many** pronunciation errors.	I have **some** pronunciation errors.	I have **few** pronunciation errors.
Citing Evidence (Opening Statement and Rebuttal)	I state my opinion **without any** evidence/details.	I support my opinion with **1-2** pieces of evidence.	I support my opinion with **many** reasons and details by citing **3 or more** pieces of evidence.
Rebuttal	I **do not** participate in the rebuttal.	I participate in the rebuttal **1-2** times.	I participate in the rebuttal **3 or more** times.
Clarity	I **cannot** explain my ideas clearly.	I can explain **some** of my ideas clearly.	I clearly explain **most** of my ideas. I demonstrate understanding of the topic.
Academic Vocabulary	I **do not** use academic vocabulary.	I use **some** academic vocabulary.	I use **many** academic vocabulary words.
Professionalism	I **never/rarely** participate respectfully in the debate, following the debate rules.	I **sometimes** participate respectfully in the debate, following the debate rules.	I **always** participate respectfully in the debate, following the debate rules.

SEL Connection

Academic conversation aligns with a variety of CASEL's SEL competencies, including communication, respect for others, social engagement, relationship building, self-efficacy, evaluating, and solving problems. Recognizing strengths in others, a subcategory under the umbrella of social awareness, can be a great SEL competency to focus on when students are doing presentations in class. Prior to the first student presentation, brainstorm a list of possible strengths with the class (e.g., good posture, clear voice, interesting visuals). After each student presents and responds to any questions, ask a student from the audience to share a strength they noticed. Encourage students to recognize and share the strength they noticed using the sentence frame "Good job! I think your strength was _____." We hope you and your students find this exercise as uplifting as we have!

Now It's Your Turn: Questions and Exercises

- What are some common misconceptions about the way SLIFE and struggling MLs develop academic conversation skills? How can teachers counteract these misconceptions?
- Observe one of your SLIFE or struggling MLs as they participate in academic conversations. Note the number of utterances they make and the complexity of those utterances. Using a three-column chart, record how many utterances are at the word level, the simple sentence level, and the complex sentence level. How can the complexity of these utterances be increased?
- After implementing one of the strategies discussed in this chapter, reflect on what went well and what could be improved.

2

Creating Aha Moments: Developing Reading Comprehension Skills

The challenges that SLIFE and other struggling MLs face with developing literacy skills can seem insurmountable, especially since many of these students are older than their peers. Generally speaking, students in the United States learn how to read at very young ages, but a growing portion of our MLs come with limited or often-times nonexistent reading skills even in their native languages. Educators are forced to address these age gaps while also catering to the needs of students who are ready for a faster pace and more challenging tasks. This chapter focuses on reading comprehension strategies specifically designed to help SLIFE and struggling MLs interact with fiction and nonfiction texts in all phases of the reading process.

Our approach incorporates several best practices for reading comprehension instruction. In our work with SLIFE and other struggling MLs, we have been guided by principles derived from the science of reading, which holds that reading instruction should emphasize foundational skills such as phonemic awareness, phonics, and decoding in addition to vocabulary, fluency, and comprehension. As the Reading League and National Committee for Effective Literacy (2023) note, this approach allows students "to acquire the alphabetic principle and learn to decode text accurately, automatically, and fluently—a critical foundation for proficient reading and comprehending complex texts" (p. 5). Indeed, our spiraling curriculum model (see Chapter 4) emphasizes the teaching of foundational skills and revisiting them systematically throughout the academic year. These skills include the identification, recognition, and accurate pronunciation of single consonants, consonant blends and digraphs, long and short vowel sounds, and vowel digraphs—along with homonyms, homophones, and homographs. In fact, the first lesson outlined in our unit plan (Chapter 5) involves students in developing foundational skills by practicing the consonant digraphs *sh*, *th*, and *ph*, which they encounter in many of the words in the text they analyze: "Is Technology Making Our Lives Better or Worse?"

Research also indicates that emphasizing oral language development alongside reading comprehension helps students draw meaning from what they read rather than just decoding the text (Reading League & National Committee for Effective Literacy, 2023). In a similar vein, Wilson (2021) underscores the importance of engaging students in academic talk and structured opportunities. As the instructional templates included in this chapter show (e.g., reading comprehension template, true/false–evidence from text template), oral language development has been our focus as we involve students in analyzing text.

We have based our reading comprehension strategies on best practices suggested by the Wilson Reading System (2021) and the CREDE Report (Genesee et al., 2006), but our goal is not to implement any one reading approach with fidelity; rather, it is to bring together the most effective elements of various frameworks. At the same time, we urge educators not to fall into the trap of believing that skills must be "drilled and killed" until mastery. In our practice, we have found that even highly successful MLs can struggle with pronunciation and spelling due to first-language interference. However, such errors do not detract them from understanding and explaining the text at hand, which is most important. Taking an asset-based mindset toward reading instruction means honoring student progress over perfection.

In addition, the strategies included in this chapter make use of several research-based guidelines for working with adolescent SLIFE. Drawing on the available literature (Benseman, 2014; Birman & Tran, 2017; Cohan & Honigsfeld, 2017; DeCapua & Marshall, 2010; Hos, 2016; Li & Zhang, 2004; Montero et al., 2014; Symons & Bian, 2022; Tigert et al., 2021; Windle & Miller, 2012, 2019), Filimon (2023) notes that the most effective strategies for adolescent SLIFE

- Engage students in meaningful learning experiences.
- Systematically integrate scaffolding techniques.
- Emphasize cooperative learning.
- Combine oral interaction with the written word.
- Integrate redundancy.
- Recycle concepts, structures, and tasks.
- Integrate routines.
- Use adapted text.
- Ensure adequate monitoring and feedback.

As readers are aware, meeting the demands of the Common Core State Standards (CCSS) is crucial to students' academic success. The CCSS for English Language Arts and Literacy include a focus on interacting with informational texts to support students in systematically developing knowledge about the world (National Governors Association Center for Best Practices, Council of Chief State School Officers, 2010). However, unlike their mainstream and ML counterparts, SLIFE can sometimes face increased obstacles due to their struggle with basic academic skills and concepts, content knowledge, and critical thinking skills. Addressing the demands of the CCSS can be a daunting undertaking for many educators, especially at the secondary level, due to the scarcity of resources specifically designed for adolescent SLIFE. In addition, the few resources available often lack rigor. For many SLIFE, exposure to informational text is seriously delayed, hindering their prospects of successfully passing standardized tests and obtaining their high school diplomas (DeCapua & Marshall, 2011b; Wright, 2015).

This chapter demonstrates vocabulary and text analysis strategies that have proven to be effective with SLIFE and other struggling MLs. Readers will become familiar with scaffolds for vocabulary acquisition as well as strategies for accessing and interacting with texts. These strategies enable SLIFE and other struggling MLs to demonstrate higher-order thinking skills through linguistic or nonlinguistic means, such as stating the textual evidence or pointing to it in the text, as demonstrated by our colleague Sarah Cordero (personal communication, November 4, 2014). Specific attention will be given to integrating the four language domains in activities that enable SLIFE to develop content knowledge and academic vocabulary.

The strategies in this chapter can all be used in conjunction with relevant and accessible texts. You will notice we use a two-column format coupled with embedded sentence frames for the templates; such a format is highly effective in engaging learners in cooperative learning opportunities that allow them to combine oral interaction with the written word. Moreover, in accordance with the research, these strategies are predicated on the use of redundancy and routines as well as on the recycling of tasks, concepts, and skills. The strategies also allow for effective monitoring and feedback by educators.

Infusing Phonics Strategies in Reading Instruction

"First we learn to read, then we read to learn." This common expression touches on a balance that all educators of struggling MLs seek to strike between teaching foundational reading strategies and focusing on reading comprehension and analysis. The good news is that, when it comes to MLs, literacy development and reading comprehension can be strengthened simultaneously. As Goldenberg (2011) explains, "Students who are not proficient in English can still learn critical reading skills and concepts in English *as they learn English*" (p. 10).

Our approach is to foster reading comprehension skills while at the same time utilizing a range of general phonics strategies that can be interspersed throughout a lesson. We have found the general phonics strategies in this chapter to be particularly effective with struggling MLs and SLIFE. These are not meant to be standalone strategies, although they may be used that way in intervention-style settings. Rather, these strategies are meant to be sprinkled throughout your lessons when students are encountering new vocabulary words, analyzing a text, or responding to reading comprehension questions. We hope that they'll inspire many aha moments among your students.

Sound Tapping

Sound tapping to segment words is a strategy often used in phonics instruction, whereby students separate each sound before blending them back together. As Wilson (2021) notes, "Sound tapping provides tactile input (or touch) to the fingertips and aids in the blending process" (p. 111). For example, the word *sit* has three sounds: /s/ /i/ /t/. To tap the word out, we would tap our index finger and thumb for the sound /s/, followed by our middle finger and thumb for /i/, followed by our ring finger and thumb for /t/. Then we'd run our thumb across all three fingers while blending the sounds back together. Tapping can also be an effective way to help MLs master digraphs such as /ch/, /sh/, and /th/, word pairs that require only one "tap" apiece. The word *shape*, for example, would be tapped out as /sh/ /ā/ /p/. Tapping is an interactive and memorable way to empower students to sound out unfamiliar words on their own: "This multisensory approach, with tactile input through the fingertips, assists students with phoneme blending" (Wilson, 2021, p. 17).

Scooping

Underlining or "scooping" syllables is a visual way to help MLs break multisyllabic words up into smaller segments that they can more readily read and pronounce. Syllabication rules can vary greatly from language to language, and scooping can help MLs recognize patterns for breaking down longer English words into smaller, more manageable syllables, helping them to figure them out.

A word such as *website* would be divided into two syllables:

website

A word such as *uncommon* would be divided into three syllables:

uncommon

Dictation as a Check for Understanding

Using dictation exercises as closing activities or "exit tickets" is a simple way not only to check for understanding but also to build students' encoding, or spelling, skills. As Wilson (2021) explains, "By working with words in two directions (decoding and encoding), you further reinforce the structures to be learned" (p. 15). Our dictation exercises usually consist of reading aloud three words and two sentences. The teacher reads aloud the words and sentences, and the students simply write what they hear. Here is an example of dictation used as an exit ticket in the case of a lesson focused on *y* as a vowel: (1) *cry*; (2) *penny*; (3) *dry*; (4) *The bunny is shy.*; (5) *The fly likes jelly.* Feedback should be given as quickly as possible either by the teacher or by allowing students to correct any errors.

Identifying Prefixes and Suffixes

Learning common prefixes and suffixes deepens students' understanding of vocabulary and helps them decode unfamiliar words independently. After all, the four most frequent prefixes (*dis-, ir-, re-, un-*) and suffixes (*-ed, -es, -ing, -ly*) account for 97 percent of all prefixed and suffixed words (Honig et al., 2008).

Bring students' attention to prefixes or suffixes when preteaching vocabulary or when they encounter an unfamiliar word in a text. Consider having them log the prefixes and suffixes they learn on a notebook page or displaying common prefixes and suffixes on a word wall. Discuss the meaning of the prefix using examples (e.g., explain that *dis-* means "not," as in *dislike*, *distrust*, and *disrespect*).

Pairing Fiction and Nonfiction

The idea of extending students' background knowledge and vocabulary by pairing fiction and nonfiction caught our attention during a presentation by Doug Lemov at Harvard University's Sontag Professional Development seminar in 2017. After reading from a children's novel about a lovable canine, Lemov tasked us with reading an informational text about the history of domesticating dogs. Although this latter text would likely have had us yawning with boredom in another context, when paired in this way it was suddenly compelling, meaningful, and informative. As Lemov (2016) notes, "Reading secondary nonfiction texts in combination with a primary text almost certainly increases the absorption rate of students reading that text" (p. 123). Immediately following Lemov's presentation, we began discussing ways to pair fiction and nonfiction in our units.

In our ELD classes, we have strategically paired texts on a range of topics, from identity to inspirational figures to environmental issues. In some cases, the texts we use are truly fiction and nonfiction; in other cases, they fall into different formats or genres. We have found that what is most important is strategic planning and exposing students to various types of texts that connect to a central theme. Here are a few of the text pairings we've used successfully with SLIFE and struggling MLs:

- To explore identity, friendship, and responsibility, we paired an adapted version of Judith Ortiz Cofer's short story "A Job for Valentín" (1995) with nonfiction texts and infographics related to bullying, peer pressure, and neurodiversity.
- For a unit aligned with the central theme of inspiration, we paired biographies of inspirational sports figures with mathematical word problems related to sports statistics. Solving word problems related

to batting averages and converting miles per hour to feet per second became more interesting, relevant, and less daunting after reading about David Ortiz's challenges and achievements.

- To explore the impact of human activity on the environment, we paired informational texts on the pros and cons of petroleum extraction with excerpts from fictional characters affected by the practice (e.g., an ecologist, a CEO, a mother, a fisherman, a truck driver).

- As part of an initiative unit focused on the Access to Clean Water Model Curriculum Unit developed by the Massachusetts Department of Elementary and Secondary Education's (2016) Next Generation ELD Project, we paired an excerpt from Robin Hill and Charles O. Hall's memoir *Just Add Water* (2012) with infographics from the World Health Organization.

Vocabulary Turn-and-Talk

The Why

Vocabulary acquisition can be made more effective for SLIFE and other struggling MLs when educators integrate opportunities for collaboration and oral interaction. As DeCapua and Marshall (2011b) note, oral interaction has been shown to serve as an effective scaffold for vocabulary acquisition among SLIFE. Our vocabulary turn-and-talk template (Figure 2.1) requires students to work in pairs and discuss their thinking as they analyze vocabulary words.

The What

The template can be used in conjunction with our graphic organizer based on the Frayer model (Figure 2.2). We typically include the word, definition, translation, picture, example, and question on the organizer and ask students to answer the question in their own words (either orally or in writing). We agree with Echevarría and colleagues' (2004) recommendation that teachers help students "review and practice words in nonprint ways" (p. 146), such as by having them draw a picture to depict a new word. Similarly, we agree with their recommendation that teachers clarify key concepts in their native language. After teachers introduce each word using the graphic organizer based on the Frayer model, they should allow students to interact with their partners using the template. When they are done analyzing each word, student pairs share their dialogue with the whole class.

The How

This strategy can be used in any activities involving vocabulary acquisition.

Materials

- Vocabulary turn-and-talk template (Figure 2.1)
- Graphic organizer based on the Frayer model (Figure 2.2)
- Presentation platform (e.g., Google Slides, PowerPoint) to display Frayer model vocabulary slides (optional)

Reading Comprehension Template

The Why

Our reading comprehension template (Figure 2.3) allows for more student interactions and higher engagement during all phases of the reading process, which is crucial when working with SLIFE and other struggling MLs. It also prompts deliberate and strategic questioning, aligned to the specific objectives of the lesson, while at the same time acting as a formative assessment tool for checking understanding. Prior to this approach, we would often come up with reading comprehension questions on the fly during text analysis, but we did not have a systematic approach for making these questions visible for students. Instead, it was a "popcorn-style" discussion, by which we asked a reading comprehension

FIGURE 2.1

Vocabulary Turn-and-Talk Template

Student A	Student B
1. How do you say _____ in your native language?	[Translate:] _____.
2. What does _____ mean?	[Define:] It means _____.
3. What can you see in this picture?	I can see _____. I observe _____.
4. Can you give me an example?	For example, [Read example:] _____.
5. [Read question:] _____?	[Answer question:] _____.

Note: This template should be used in conjunction with the adapted Frayer model graphic organizer.

FIGURE 2.2

Graphic Organizer Based on the Frayer Model

Definition: Devices used to solve problems	Picture
Example from text: Technology impacts our lives every day.	**Question:** What types of technology do you use every day? **Answer:** I use _____.

Technology

Translation: _____

question orally and one student responded at a time. By contrast, having the template handy and creating the questions and—importantly, the sentence stems—in advance has allowed us to make the process more meaningful for all students to participate, not only a select few. There are, of course, situations in which a generic reading comprehension template can be used, such as the one for tackling math problems (Figure 2.6).

When employing this strategy for the first time, consider asking simple, direct questions such as those shown in Figure 2.4 so students can get acquainted with the new format using familiar language and content. As students gain familiarity with the template, you can increase the rigor of the questions by asking students to make inferences, compare and contrast, and so on, as shown in Figures 2.3 and 2.5.

In direct contrast to the one-size-fits-all approach of general sentence stems, the reading comprehension template allows educators to differentiate instruction in mixed-level classrooms, provides specific scaffolding for textual analysis, and connects the four language domains in one activity. Students are supposed to read the text, write their answers to questions, and share their responses with a partner. As you look at the examples in Figure 2.4, note that some of the sentence stems, such as those for citing textual evidence (e.g., *According to the text*...), are recycled. We make an effort to recycle academic language throughout the four language domains in each activity—as demonstrated by the various templates included here—to help students internalize it. It brings us great joy to hear students using phrases such as *based on the text* and *from my perspective* in class without prompting. That's when we know they got it!

The What

Teachers should create text-based questions and include them in the Student A column of the reading comprehension template when designing their own materials. For each question selected, teachers should include an accompanying sentence stem that students can use as they construct their answer. These sentence stems should be provided in the

Student B column. When modeling how to use this resource, draw students' attention to the evidence in the text that supports their answer. Echevarría and colleagues (2004) recommend using a variety of question types, with particular emphasis on those that promote the development of higher-order thinking skills. An example of such questions are those included in the generic reading comprehension template for tackling math problems (Figure 2.6).

We like to pair the reading comprehension template with the slide-and-glide strategy. In this exercise, students are organized into two lines facing each other and discuss the first question on the template with the person directly across from them. Each student should both ask and answer the question. When everyone is done, students in one of the lines "slide and glide" over one position so they are now facing a new partner, with whom they discuss the second question. The process repeats as needed until all questions on the template have been asked. (The concentric circles strategy is an effective variation of this activity.) In this way, the template becomes a speaking tool for reading aloud content-area vocabulary and interacting with peers.

The How

This strategy can be used in any activities involving text analysis.

Materials

- Text/reading selection
- Reading Comprehension Template (Figure 2.3)

True/False–Evidence from Text Template

The Why

The true/false–evidence from text template (Figure 2.7) allows SLIFE and struggling MLs to demonstrate their critical thinking while reading. During textual analysis, students evaluate text-based statements and identify those that support their answer by pointing to and/or reading

FIGURE 2.3

Reading Comprehension Template

Student A	Student B
1. What is the title of the text?	The title of the text is _____.
2. Why is the impact of technology controversial?	The impact of technology is controversial because _____.
3. Why are people excited about technology?	People are excited about technology because _____ _____.
4. Why are people concerned about technology?	People are concerned about technology because _____ _____.

FIGURE 2.4

Sample Reading Comprehension Template #1

Student A	Student B
1. Based on the text, which animals are herbivores?	Based on the text, the following animals are herbivores: *deer and rabbits.*
2. What textual evidence can you use in support of your answer to question 1?	According to the text, "Animals like *deer and rabbits only eat plants.*"
3. According to the text, which animals are carnivores?	According to the text, the following animals are carnivores: *wolves and lions.*
4. What textual evidence can you use in support of your answer to question 3?	According to the text, "Animals like *wolves and lions eat plant-eating animals.*"

FIGURE 2.5

Sample Reading Comprehension Template #2

Student A	Student B
What is the difference between commensalism and mutualism?	**The difference between commensalism and mutualism is that** in commensalism, one organism is helped, while in mutualism, both organisms gain from the relationship.
What is the difference between mutualism and parasitism?	**The difference between mutualism and parasitism is that** in mutualism, both organisms gain from the relationship, while in parasitism, one organism is helped but the host is harmed.
What is the difference between parasitism and predation?	**The difference between parasitism and predation is that** in parasitism, one organism is helped but its host is harmed, while predation refers to an animal that hunts and eats other animals for food.
How can prey animals avoid predators?	**Prey animals can avoid predators by** hiding.

Note: Responses correspond to texts "Symbiosis" and "Predators and Their Prey" from T. Collins and M. J. Maples, 2008, *Gateway to Science*, pp. 88–89. Thomson Heinle.

them. This strategy addresses the CCSS's focus on citing textual evidence to support claims and interacting with peers using complex academic discourse.

The What

Teachers should craft text-based statements and include them in the first column of the template. Students then analyze the statements and decide if they are true or false, justifying their answers using textual evidence. In the second column, students write their responses using the sentence frames provided at the top of the template. Students can complete the activity as a turn-and-talk or a think-write-pair-share exercise. As with the reading comprehension template, teachers can follow

FIGURE 2.6

Sample Reading Comprehension Template #3

Student A	Student B
What does the problem tell us?	The problem tells us that _____.
What does the problem ask us to solve? What are we looking for?	The problem asks us to _____.
What kind of information is relevant?	The relevant information is _____.
How did you solve the problem? What did you do first?	First, I _____.
What did you do second?	Second, I _____.
That's interesting. Please keep going!	_____.
OK, so you are saying that first, you _____, and then, you _____.	Right. Does this make sense to you?

Echevarría and colleagues' (2004) recommendation to use a variety of statement types, especially those that promote the development of higher-order thinking skills. (See Figures 2.8 and 2.9 for completed examples of the template adapted to different content areas.)

FIGURE 2.7

True/False–Evidence from Text Template

Statement	True/False–Evidence from Text
1. Cell phones and cars are examples of technology we use every day.	Ex.: This is true because the text says, "When we use our cell phones, drive our cars, or use our computers, we are using technology."
2. Everyone agrees that technology is beneficial to our lives.	This is _____ because the text says, _____ _____ _____ _____ _____ _____
3. Technology can make communication with people we love quicker.	This is _____ because the text says, _____ _____ _____ _____ _____ _____
4. Driving cars is better for the environment.	This is _____ because the text says, _____ _____ _____ _____ _____ _____

FIGURE 2.8

Sample True/False–Evidence from Text Template #1

Statement	True/False–Evidence from Text
Ex.: Not all living things need nutrients.	*Ex.:* This is false because the text says, *"All living things take in nutrients to stay alive."*
1. Plants are consumers.	This is false because the text says, *"Plants are the first food-makers, or producers, in an ecosystem."*
2. Humans are producers because they can make their own food.	This is false because the text says, *"Animals cannot make food from sunlight."*
3. Wolves and lions are called secondary consumers because they like to eat a second time.	This is false because the text says, *"Animals like wolves and lions eat plant-eating animals. This makes them secondary consumers."*
4. Primary consumers can eat plants or other animals.	This is true because the text says, *"Animals like deer and rabbits only eat plants. They are called primary consumers."*
5. Decomposers include rotting wood, leaves, and stems.	This is false because the text says, *"Decomposers turn dead plants and animals into their own food energy so they keep nutrients moving through the ecosystem."*

Note: Responses correspond to an excerpt by E. Duran, J. Gusman, and J. Shefelbine, 2005, *ACCESS to Science*. Great Source Education Group.

FIGURE 2.9

Sample True/False–Evidence from Text Template #2

Statement	True/False–Evidence from Text
Ex: Lines and angles form figures all around us.	This is true because the text says, "Lines and angles are all around you. They form the basic shapes of many things."
1. Intersecting lines never meet.	This is false because the text says, "Lines that cross are intersecting lines."
2. Parallel lines are in the same plane.	This is true because the text says, "Parallel lines lie in the same plane but never intersect."
3. Skew lines meet to form a right angle.	This is false because the text says, "Two lines that do not lie in the same plane are called skew lines."
4. Acute angles are less than 90 degrees.	This is true because the text says, "Acute angle: $0° < x < 90°$."
5. Obtuse angles are exactly 90 degrees.	This is false because the text says, "Obtuse angle: $90° < y < 180°$."

Note: Responses correspond to an excerpt by E. Duran, J. Gusman, and J. Shefelbine, 2005, *ACCESS to Math*. Great Source Education Group.

The How

As in the case of the previous template, this tool can be used in the analysis of any type of text, during a read-aloud, or as an independent activity, followed by sharing in pairs.

Materials

- Text/reading selection
- True/false–evidence from text template (Figure 2.7).

SEL Connection

When thinking about ways to integrate SEL into your lesson, it may be helpful to reflect on your instructional materials, strategies, and classroom environment (Massachusetts Department of Elementary and Secondary Education, 2019). You can do this alone or with a content team or professional learning community (PLC) when developing or revising your curriculum. When selecting a text to read with your MLs, especially in a humanities lesson, be sure to examine the themes, author, and audience for possible SEL connections. Here are some questions to consider:

- What themes within the text(s) connect to one or more SEL competencies that you would like to explore further with your students?
- Do the themes within the texts you read throughout the school year address a range of the overarching SEL competencies, such as self-awareness, self-management, social responsibility, relationship skills, and responsible decision making (CASEL, 2020)?
- Do authors share a similar cultural background to your students? Do they come from different walks of life?
- Where are your students from? How old are they? What are their likes and dislikes? How will the text you choose be relevant to their lives or to their academic journeys? The more you get to know your students, the easier it is to select texts they will find relevant and interesting.

Finally, you may find, as we have, that the texts you'd like to use may need to be adapted. Although this process might be time-consuming, we have found that some small changes to the material—chunking the text, highlighting or boldfacing key vocabulary, and adding images (Cohan & Honigsfeld, 2017)—can go a long way toward making it more accessible to readers.

Now It's Your Turn: Questions and Exercises

- What are some of the challenges your students face related to reading development?
- Observe a reading lesson with SLIFE or struggling MLs. Record details of how the teacher engages these students in the lesson. Pay attention to how the students engage with the text. Take note of how many student responses demonstrate evidence of higher-order thinking (e.g., analysis, evaluation, inference).
- Use the reading comprehension template as a model to create a template of your own that addresses the needs of your SLIFE and struggling MLs. Discuss the questions that you developed, the rationale for focusing on those questions, and how you plan to use the template with students.

3

Cracking the Code:
Achieving Success in Academic Writing

A s many teachers of SLIFE are well aware, these students often possess limited or nonexistent academic writing skills, due to the severe interruptions they have experienced in their schooling or as a result of their immigration/life experiences. This daunting reality makes the idea of writing a complete sentence, let alone an essay, seem overwhelming to both students and teachers! This chapter provides an overview of our highly successful writing protocol, which we've adapted specifically for SLIFE and other struggling MLs. In addition, this chapter gives readers access to all the instructional materials that make this protocol effective, such as model responses, claim-evidence graphic organizers, and a writing rubric.

This protocol has enabled our SLIFE and other struggling MLs not only to pass the rigorous Massachusetts standardized tests but also to meet graduation requirements. The protocol is aligned with research guidelines for scaffolding academic writing in the case of MLs. As Filimon (2023) notes, these guidelines include

- Helping students identify patterns specific to U.S. academic writing (Cotterall & Cohen, 2003; DelliCarpini, 2012; Lee, 2018).
- Modeling evidence-based writing (Cotterall & Cohen, 2003; DelliCarpini, 2012; Lee, 2018; Olson et al., 2012, 2017).

- Using color coding (Kim et al., 2011; Olson et al., 2012, 2015, 2017).
- Incorporating peer and instructor feedback (Cotterall & Cohen, 2003; DelliCarpini, 2012; Olson et al., 2015, 2017).
- Using linguistic supports (Cotterall & Cohen, 2003; Kim et al., 2011; Olson et al., 2011, 2015, 2017).

Additionally, this protocol aligns with the SIOP Model recommendation that teachers provide procedural scaffolding such as using an instructional framework that includes "explicit teaching, modeling, and guided and independent practice opportunities with peers, and an expectation for independent application" (Echevarría et al., 2014, p. 124).

The CCSS for English Language Arts and Literacy emphasize using textual evidence and valid reasoning to convey complex ideas. This means writing informative and explanatory texts is highlighted over writing personal narratives and substantiating claims with one's own opinions (Wright, 2015; Zwiers et al., 2014). Such a focus presents significant challenges for SLIFE, who, in addition to having literacy needs along with gaps in educational experience, generally lack the most basic skills needed to produce formal writing. Therefore, it is imperative that educators scaffold the writing process by first unmasking the key components of academic writing before challenging students to produce evidence-based writing of their own.

This chapter demonstrates writing strategies that have proven to be effective with SLIFE and other struggling MLs at the secondary level. Readers will become familiar with a writing protocol encompassing carefully sequenced strategies that enable learners to find evidence in a text using nonlinguistic means, cite evidence from the text to evaluate text-based claims, and write a multiparagraph response featuring textual evidence.

Writing Protocol

Our writing protocol was inspired by the innovative Writing with Colors strategy developed by Allison Renna and Patrick Daly to help students successfully tackle the long-composition and open-response questions of Massachusetts's standardized ELA test (O'Toole, 2015). In this method, students use highlighters to analyze model responses by color coding the essential parts of an essay, such as topic sentences, evidence, and explanations (Daly, 2012).

We begin by selecting accessible texts. This can be easier said than done, especially in the beginning of the year, since struggling MLs can have, in some instances, no English skills and very limited literacy backgrounds in their native languages. Very often, we have to extensively adapt existing materials or even write the texts ourselves, as in the example provided in this book. Nonetheless, we believe that it is imperative to reduce the cognitive load associated with understanding complex material if we want SLIFE and other struggling MLs to focus on the analytical steps that make up the writing protocol.

Next, we create a set of four model essays (see Figures 3.1 and 3.2) in response to a text-based prompt, each written at a different level of proficiency, ranging from exemplary to failing, in line with recommendations from research (Olson et al., 2012, 2017). In general, in the case of scaffolding paragraph writing, the exemplary model response includes a topic sentence, clear explanations introduced by transition words, and supporting evidence for each explanation. The proficient response features similar explanations and supporting evidence, but the topic sentence and all transition words are omitted. The model response rated needs improvement includes only explanations without any supporting textual evidence; also, the introduction and transition words are omitted. The failing response features a lengthy response, which in reality was copied from the text on which the writing prompt was based. Since many of our SLIFE and other struggling MLs fall into the trap of responding to a text-based prompt by copying that particular text, we want to demonstrate to our students the dangers of this practice.

We then introduce the protocol color scheme to our students using our adapted writing with colors chart (Figure 3.3): pink for the topic sentences, blue for explanations, and green for quotations and other supporting textual evidence. As a whole class, we use these colors to identify the introduction and conclusion, the explanations, and the supporting evidence from the exemplary model response. Once students have grasped the components of a well-developed response, we add orange for transition words such as *first, second, additionally,* and *finally.* With the addition of the transition words, students are able to see the progression of ideas within the text.

After the initial introduction of the color scheme using the exemplary model response, we analyze the proficient response as a whole class to allow students additional guided practice. We then ask students to compare the two model responses and identify the differences between them using the adapted writing with colors chart. Students usually notice that the proficient response is missing the orange (transition words) and the pink (introduction and conclusion) and is not as clear to read as the exemplary model.

We then ask students to work in pairs to color-code the needs improvement and failing model responses. When they're done, we conduct a whole-class discussion about the differences among the four model responses revealed by the color coding. Students often note that the needs improvement response is mainly highlighted in blue, since it includes explanations but no introduction or conclusion, supporting evidence, or transition words. Some students initially believe that the failing response should be rated higher until they start color-coding it and realize that none of the colors can be used! It is valuable for students to learn that length does not necessarily translate to quality.

Our next step is to create a variety of prompts, based on the same accessible source text, so students can practice writing their own essays. Here, for example, is a prompt from a unit on identity based on two short texts from *Keys to Learning* (Chamot et al., 2013) about two students, Liliana and Pablo: "Compare and contrast Liliana's and Pablo's experiences in school. How are they similar? How are they different? Support your answer with relevant details and textual evidence." In response to this prompt, the students wrote two paragraphs: one showing the similarities between Liliana and Pablo, and the other illustrating the differences. They wrote the first paragraph as a class and the second paragraph in pairs. Then they swapped papers with their partners and used their highlighters to color-code each component: introduction/topic, explanations, evidence from text, and transition words.

Over time, we exposed students to increasingly complex texts and prompts (e.g., "Often in works of literature, characters have a mix of positive and negative traits. Describe a character's positive and negative characteristics. Support your answer with reasons and examples from the text."). We have found that consistency is crucial to ensuring SLIFE and other struggling MLs internalize the patterns of academic writing (Cartwright & Filimon, 2018). In doing this, we followed the SIOP Model recommendations (Echevarría et al., 2004), especially in terms of clear explanations of academic tasks, consistent use of scaffolding techniques, and using activities that integrate all language skills. By following this model, our students were able to produce responses ranging from one to five paragraphs in length as the year progressed. Students consistently incorporated textual evidence using quotes and provided sentence frames such as "According to the text . . . ," "Based on the text . . . ," and "As the author explains . . . ."

Model Responses

The Why

The greatest hindrance in teaching SLIFE and other struggling MLs academic writing skills is the cognitive load associated with understanding complex material, such as advanced student responses to writing prompts. Creating accessible model open-response essays to questions about the texts at various proficiency levels allows struggling MLs—especially SLIFE—to see the structure of an open-response essay and identify the components that make up a successful response (Filimon, 2023). This enables SLIFE and other struggling MLs to focus, instead, on the analytical steps that make up the writing with colors protocol, instead of battling unsuccessfully with sample responses designed for mainstream students or MLs at higher levels of English proficiency.

The What

Teachers can start by first developing a set of four model responses, showing a range of responses from exemplary to failing. As a class, teachers should engage students in analyzing the text by highlighting the first two model responses with the students' help, using the four colors (pink, blue, green, orange). As students highlight the model responses, they should be encouraged to notice the differences in quality between the two responses (students will immediately notice that some of the colors are "missing"). To promote independent learning, teachers can have the students analyze and highlight the last two model responses in pairs. We suggest that teachers include chunks of copied text in the last model response (failing), so students can understand why they do not get any credit for copied work.

The How

This strategy can be used every time a new type of writing prompt is introduced.

Materials

- Model responses (e.g., Figures 3.1, 3.2)
- Adapted writing with colors chart (Figure 3.3)
- Highlighters or colored pencils

To give readers an idea of how versatile this strategy is, we have included two sets of model responses based on the same reading, "Is Technology Making Our Lives Better or Worse?" The first set is the one we created for our SLIFE self-contained class, to be taught during the second part of the academic year (Figure 3.1). The second set can be used in mixed ELD classes, where SLIFE and other struggling MLs at higher levels of English proficiency might be enrolled (Figure 3.2).

FIGURE 3.1
Sample Model Responses #1

Prompt: How does technology impact our lives? Explain the advantages and disadvantages of technology. Give specific examples from the text to support your answer.

Exemplary

Technology impacts our lives in both positive and negative ways. Like everything, technology has both advantages and disadvantages.

There are many advantages of technology. First, we can use computers to communicate faster. According to the text, "instead of writing and mailing a letter, people can send an email from their computers." Second, we can use cell phones to talk to our friends and family from different countries. The text states, "they can now use cell phones to communicate with their friends and family, even if they live far away." Finally, we can get to school or work quicker, by car or by bus. Based on the text, "they can get to work or school easily by driving a car or taking a bus."

There are also disadvantages of technology. For example, we can get distracted if we are using our cell phones while driving. According to the text, "many accidents happen because people are distracted by their cell phones while driving." Also, we do not spend much time talking to our friends face to face. The text states, "they worry about how much time people spend using their cell phones and computers, instead of talking to their friends in person." In addition, technology can be bad for our health and the environment. Based on the text, "instead of relying on cars or buses to go short distances, people should walk or ride a bike because this is better for their health and the environment."

In conclusion, technology has many advantages and disadvantages.

Proficient

There are many advantages of technology. We can use computers to communicate faster. According to the text, "instead of writing and mailing a letter, people can send an email from their computers." We can use cell phones to talk to our friends and family from different countries. The text states, "they can now use cell phones to communicate with their friends and family, even if they live far away." We can get to school or work quicker, by car or by bus. Based on the text, "they can get to work or school easily by driving a car or taking a bus."

There are also disadvantages of technology. We can get distracted if we are using our cell phones while driving. According to the text, "many accidents happen because people are distracted by their cell phones while driving." We do not spend much time talking to our friends face to face. The text states, "they worry about how much time people spend using their cell phones and computers, instead of talking to their friends in person." Technology can be bad for our health and the environment. Based on the text, "instead of relying on cars or buses to go short distances, people should walk or ride a bike because this is better for their health and the environment."

(continued)

Figure 3.1—(*continued*)
Sample Model Responses #1

Needs Improvement

There are many advantages of technology. We can use computers to communicate faster. We can use cell phones to talk to our friends and family from different countries. We can get to school or work quicker, by car or by bus.

There are also disadvantages of technology. We can get distracted if we are using our cell phones while driving. We do not spend much time talking to our friends face to face. Technology can be bad for our health and the environment.

Failing

Technology impacts our lives every day. When we use our cell phones, drive our cars, or use our computers, we are using technology. However, whether technology is making our lives better or worse is a controversial issue.

Many people are excited about using technology because they think it makes everyday activities faster. For example, instead of writing and mailing a letter, people can send an email from their computers. Also, they can now use cell phones to communicate with their friends and family, even if they live far away. In addition, they can get to work or school easily by driving a car or taking a bus.

Other people are concerned about the use of technology because they think it can be distracting and even dangerous. They say that many accidents happen because people are distracted by their cell phones while driving. Also, they worry about how much time people spend using their cell phones and computers, instead of talking to their friends in person. Finally, they believe that instead of relying on cars or buses to go short distances, people should walk or ride a bike because this is better for their health and the environment.

Figure 3.2
Sample Model Responses #2

Prompt: Compare and contrast the advantages and disadvantages of technology. Give specific examples from the text to support your answer.

Exemplary

Technology impacts our lives every day. Like everything, technology has both advantages and disadvantages.

First, technology impacts our lives in a positive way because we can communicate with each other faster. According to the text, "instead of writing and mailing a letter, people can send an email from their computers." However, if people use computers too much, they don't have time to talk to their friends face to face. Based on the text, "they worry about how much time people spend using their cell phones and computers, instead of talking to their friends."

Second, technology has a positive impact on our lives because we can talk to family and friends who live in a different country. The text states, "they can now use cell phones to communicate with their friends and family, even if they live far away." On the other hand, using cell phones can be very dangerous, because it can cause accidents. According to the author, "many accidents happen because people are distracted by their cell phones while driving."

Finally, technology has a positive impact on our lives because we can get where we want quicker. Based on the text, "they can get to work or school easily by driving a car or taking a bus." Nevertheless, cars and buses can have a negative impact on people's health and the environment by causing illnesses and more pollution. According to the text, "instead of relying on cars and buses, people should walk or ride a bike because this is better for their health or the environment."

In conclusion, there are many advantages and disadvantages of using technology. Technology impacts our lives in both positive and negative ways.

Proficient

Technology impacts our lives every day. Like everything, technology has both advantages and disadvantages.

Technology impacts our lives in a positive way because we can communicate with each other faster. According to the text, "instead of writing and mailing a letter, people can send an email from their computers." If people use computers too much, they don't have time to talk to their friends face to face. Based on the text, "they worry about how much time people spend using their cell phones and computers, instead of talking to their friends."

Technology has a positive impact on our lives because we can talk to family and friends who live in a different country. The text states, "they can now use cell phones to communicate with their friends and family, even if they live far away." Using cell phones can be very dangerous, because it can cause accidents. According to the author, "many accidents happen because people are distracted by their cell phones while driving."

Technology has a positive impact on our lives because we can get where we want quicker. Based on the text, "they can get to work or school easily by driving a car or taking a bus." Cars and buses can have a negative impact on people's health and the environment by causing illnesses and more pollution. According to the text, "instead of relying on cars and buses, people should walk or ride a bike because this is better for their health or the environment."

Needs Improvement

Technology impacts our lives in a positive way because we can communicate with each other faster. If people use computers too much, they don't have time to talk to their friends face to face.

Technology has a positive impact on our lives because we can talk to family and friends who live in a different country. Using cell phones can be very dangerous, because it can cause accidents.

Technology has a positive impact on our lives because we can get where we want quicker. Cars and buses can have a negative impact on people's health and the environment by causing illnesses and more pollution.

Failing

Technology impacts our lives every day. When we use our cell phones, drive our cars, or use our computers, we are using technology. However, whether technology is making our lives better or worse is a controversial issue.

Many people are excited about using technology because they think it makes everyday activities faster. For example, instead of writing and mailing a letter, people can send an email from their computers. Also, they can now use cell phones to communicate with their friends and family, even if they live far away. In addition, they can get to work or school easily by driving a car or taking a bus.

(continued)

FIGURE 3.2—*(continued)*

Sample Model Responses #2

Other people are concerned about the use of technology because they think it can be distracting and even dangerous. They say that many accidents happen because people are distracted by their cell phones while driving. Also, they worry about how much time people spend using their cell phones and computers, instead of talking to their friends in person. Finally, they believe that instead of relying on cars or buses to go short distances, people should walk or ride a bike because this is better for their health and the environment.

Adapted Writing with Colors Framework

The Why

Although mainstream students and MLs at higher levels of English proficiency may struggle at times with the patterns of academic writing, SLIFE encounter the added challenge of lacking familiarity with the basic components of academic writing, let alone the patterns. The adapted writing with colors framework enables SLIFE to first identify the components of academic writing (topic sentence, transition words, explanations, and textual evidence) through a color-coding process, thus relying on nonverbal cues. As research emphasizes (Kim et al., 2011; Olson et al., 2012, 2015, 2017), color-coding enables not only SLIFE but also MLs in general to move from understanding these components to recognizing patterns specific to U.S. academic writing.

The What

Students refer to the adapted writing with colors framework as they analyze model responses or construct their own responses to writing prompts. Teachers should provide students with examples of basic transition words (e.g., *first, second, finally*) as well as sentence stems for citing textual evidence (e.g., *According to the text, Based on the text, The text says*). Teachers may encourage students to add more transition words and examples of textual evidence sentence stems as they progress in mastering the adapted writing with colors framework. We have included two versions of the adapted writing with colors chart: one for teachers and one for students to complete and use as an ongoing reference (Figure 3.3). Each time students are given a writing prompt, we encourage them to refer back to this chart. Students can continually add to the transition words section as they increase their academic vocabulary.

The How

This framework can be used in any type of activity involving analyzing writing samples or responding to writing prompts.

Materials

- Adapted writing with colors chart (Figure 3.3)
- Highlighters or colored pencils

Claim-Evidence Graphic Organizer

The Why

Producing writing that features textual evidence to support one's claims can be overwhelming for any student, but especially for SLIFE and other struggling MLs. For educators, teaching students the patterns of academic writing through traditional graphic organizers may feel like daunting work, especially as they prepare their SLIFE and other struggling MLs for high-stakes tests to meet graduation requirements. The complexity of such organizers can interfere with students' ability to produce an effective written response to a prompt, especially in the case of writing multiparagraph essays.

The What

Our easy-to-use claim-evidence graphic organizer (Figure 3.4)—created to complement Technology Model Response Set 1—is specifically designed to align with our writing protocol and incorporates familiar elements and sentence stems from the reading comprehension and the true/false–evidence from text templates. To scaffold paragraph organization,

FIGURE 3.3

Adapted Writing with Colors Chart: Teacher's Guide

Topic Sentences (highlight in PINK)	• Key words from writing prompt • Introduction • Conclusion • Topic sentences • Answer to the prompt
Transition Words (highlight in ORANGE)	• *First* • *Second* • *After* • *Additionally* • *Also*
Explanation (highlight in BLUE)	Explanations in the writer's own words
Textual Evidence (highlight in GREEN)	• *According to the text,* • *Based on the text,* • *The text says,* • *The text states,* • *According to the author,* • Quotations and paraphrased examples from the text

Note: Based on "The Essence of Innovation: Uncovering the Conditions Essential for Innovative Instructional Practice," by P. Daly, 2012. Adapted with permission.

Adapted Writing with Colors Chart: Student's Guide

Topic Sentences (highlight in PINK)	
Transition Words (highlight in ORANGE)	
Explanation (highlight in BLUE)	
Textual Evidence (highlight in GREEN)	

Note: Based on "The Essence of Innovation: Uncovering the Conditions Essential for Innovative Instructional Practice," by P. Daly, 2012. Adapted with permission.

teachers should explain that the information in the second row will be used for the introduction. In the first body paragraph, students should use the information from the first sentence stem (*"There are many advantages of . . ."*) as the topic sentence. Then they will use the information in the first column (which includes explanations/claims), introduced by the transition words. Body paragraph 1 should also include the corresponding textual evidence (third column), followed by a "closing" sentence. Body paragraph 2 should feature explanations or claims introduced by transition words (and the corresponding evidence). Finally, students should end their essay with a conclusion (information in the bottom row).

When using this graphic organizer with our students, we usually present the sentence stem portion in color, following the adapted writing with colors color scheme. We use pink for the sentence stems associated with the introduction, topic sentences, "closing" sentences, and conclusion. Blue is used for the sentence stems that scaffold claims, which are introduced by orange transition words. Finally, we use green for the third column (textual evidence).

The How

This graphic organizer can be used as a scaffold in any type of activity involving responding to writing prompts.

Materials

- Claim-evidence graphic organizer (Figure 3.4)
- Highlighters or colored pencils

Writing Rubric

The Why

Most rubrics available for general implementation, especially at the high school level, do not include indicators applicable to students at the lowest levels of English proficiency. Therefore, many educators feel unprepared and confused about how to score these students' writing,

FIGURE 3.4

Claim-Evidence Graphic Organizer

Prompt: How do various technological items impact our lives? Explain the advantages and disadvantages of one technological device (e.g., cell phone, GPS, computer). Justify your opinion with specific examples and textual evidence from the text we read in class and your own research.	
Introduction	Technology impacts our lives in both positive and negative ways. I use _____ for _____. (name of technological device)
Body Paragraph 1	There are many advantages of _____.

First, _____	According to the text, _____

Second, _____	The text states, _____

Finally, _____	Based on the text, _____

As you can see, there are many benefits to using _____.

Body Paragraph 2	There are also disadvantages of _____.

For example, _____	According to the text, _____

Also, _____	The text states, _____

In addition, _____	Based on the text, _____

Therefore, there are many drawbacks to _____.

Conclusion	In conclusion, _____ has both advantages and disadvantages. In my opinion, there are more _____ because _____

especially when grades are due. Our citing textual evidence writing rubric (Figure 3.5) helps address these concerns.

The What

Teachers should introduce the rubric during the analysis of the model responses to show students how their answers will be scored. Although the rubric is written in first person, it is intended to be used by teachers for scoring purposes. We have found that this student-friendly language makes the rubric accessible to students when faced with understanding their feedback. We would like to emphasize that it is also a good idea to have students score model responses against the rubric to ensure they understand the scoring criteria. Once students have a clear understanding of the rubric, they can be taught how to use it to score their own writing as well.

The How

This rubric can be used for assessing any type of writing response that includes textual evidence. Feel free to adapt the rubric for your own assessment purposes; for example, you may want to omit the textual evidence criteria if you use the rubric to assess personal narratives. You can see a completed sample version of the rubric in Figure 3.6. For peer editing, ask your students to switch essays with a partner and assess them using the rubric. Encourage students to provide feedback with sentence frames like *You are missing . . . , I think you need more . . . ,* and *Great job on your . . . !*

Materials

- Citing textual evidence writing rubric (Figure 3.5)

SEL Connection

Writing is typically an independent task, but we have found that our protocol enables students to collaborate, give constructive feedback, and

FIGURE 3.5

Citing Textual Evidence Writing Rubric

	Level 1 (1 point)	Level 2 (2 points)	Level 3 (3 points)
Topic Sentence	**No topic sentence is present.**	I can write an **incomplete topic sentence** for each body paragraph OR I can write **some** complete topic sentences.	I can write a **complete topic sentence** for each body paragraph.
Transition Words	I can use **0–1 adequate transition words** in each body paragraph.	I can use **2 adequate transition words** in each body paragraph.	I can use **at least 2 appropriate transition words** in each body paragraph.
Explanations	I can include **0–1 adequate explanations** in each body paragraph.	I can include **2 adequate explanations** in each body paragraph.	I can include **at least 2 appropriate explanations** in each body paragraph.
Textual Evidence	I can include **0–1 pieces of adequate textual evidence** in each body paragraph.	I can include **2 pieces of adequate textual evidence** in each body paragraph.	I can include **at least 2 pieces of appropriate textual evidence** in each body paragraph.
Organization	I can write **words** and **simple phrases**.	I can write **phrases** and **short** sentences.	I can write **simple** and **expanded** sentences with **details**, including an introduction and a conclusion.
Grammar and Punctuation	**Many errors** make my writing very hard to understand.	**Some errors** make my writing hard to understand.	My writing is easy to understand because it has **few errors**.
Word Choice	I can use **simple social** and **academic** vocabulary.	I can use **general academic** vocabulary.	I can use general and **some specific academic** vocabulary.
Response to Task	I can answer **one part** of the prompt.	I can answer **parts** of the prompt.	I can answer the prompt **completely**.

Note: Based on *WIDA Writing Rubric, Grades 1–12*, 2020, Board of Regents of the University of Wisconsin System.

Score: _____ /24 = _____ %

Notes:

FIGURE 3.6

Sample Completed Citing Textual Evidence Writing Rubric

	Level 1 (1 point)	Level 2 (2 points)	Level 3 (3 points)
Topic Sentence	**No topic sentence is present**.	I can write an **incomplete topic sentence** for each body paragraph OR I can write **some** complete topic sentences.	I can write a **complete topic sentence** for each body paragraph.
Transition Words	I can use **0–1 adequate transition words** in each body paragraph.	I can use **2 adequate transition words** in each body paragraph.	I can use **at least 2 appropriate transition words** in each body paragraph.
Explanations	I can include **0–1 adequate explanations** in each body paragraph.	I can include **2 adequate explanations** in each body paragraph.	I can include **at least 2 appropriate explanations** in each body paragraph.
Textual Evidence	I can include **0–1 pieces of adequate textual evidence** in each body paragraph.	I can include **2 pieces of adequate textual evidence** in each body paragraph.	I can include **at least 2 pieces of appropriate textual evidence** in each body paragraph.
Organization	I can write **words** and **simple phrases**.	I can write **phrases** and **short sentences**.	I can write **simple** and **expanded** sentences with **details**, including an introduction and a conclusion.
Grammar and Punctuation	**Many errors** make my writing very hard to understand.	**Some errors** make my writing hard to understand.	My writing is easy to understand because it has **few errors**.
Word Choice	I can use **simple social** and **academic** vocabulary.	I use **general academic** vocabulary.	I use general and **some specific academic** vocabulary.
Response to Task	I can answer **one part** of the prompt.	I can answer **parts** of the prompt.	I can answer the prompt **completely**.

Note: Based on *WIDA Writing Rubric, Grades 1–12*, 2020, Board of Regents of the University of Wisconsin System.

Score: 21/24 = 88%

Notes:

(continued)

FIGURE 3.6—(*continued*)

Sample Completed Citing Textual Evidence Writing Rubric

Topic sentence: *Good headings ("advantages" and "disadvantages"), but you need to include complete topic sentences.*

Transition words: *Well done! Your transition words strengthen your essay.*

Explanation: *Great job explaining the advantages and disadvantages!*

Textual evidence: *Good job citing evidence from the text—but be sure that your evidence and explanation are directly connected.*

Organization: *Excellent job organizing your essay!*

Grammar and punctuation: *Use appropriate past tense verb forms.*

Word choice: *Good use of unit-related vocabulary words (pros, cons, device, safety).*

Response to task: *Great work explaining both the positives and negatives of technology as well as your personal opinion. Well done!*

work cooperatively with others—all essential components in relationship building (CASEL, 2020)—during the peer editing phase. In the past, prior to implementing our adapted writing with colors protocol, peer editing was a fruitless, often frustrating, task. Students would attempt to edit one another's responses and would even at times create new errors instead of resolving existing ones! However, after implementing our protocol, we have found that the process of switching and "coloring" peer responses was an effective way not only to improve student writing but also to build important SEL skills.

Now It's Your Turn: Questions and Exercises

- How do you scaffold writing for your SLIFE and/or struggling MLs? What challenges have you encountered while implementing these scaffolds?
- Using the sample responses presented in this chapter as a guide, develop four model responses tailored to the needs of your SLIFE and/or struggling MLs. Use color coding to identify the components of academic writing.

- Collect one or more writing samples from your students and use the citing textual evidence rubric to assess them. With a partner, discuss strengths and areas of improvement in student writing. Determine instructional strategies that would address the areas in need of improvement.

4

"I Think I Got It Now!"
A Spiraling Approach to Instruction

Implementing a rigorous curriculum aligned with the demands of state standards is crucial to students' academic success, particularly at the secondary level. However, this can be a seemingly insurmountable task for teachers of SLIFE and other struggling MLs, especially as schools try to cope with the reality of ongoing enrollment. Now equipped with a toolbox of strategies, readers will learn how to maximize their effectiveness by rethinking traditional approaches to instruction. This chapter presents our spiraling curriculum model (Figure 4.1), which has proven successful with MLs at the secondary level across content areas. We first implemented this model eight years ago at the school where we worked at the time: an urban newcomer program in Massachusetts that served between 200 and 300 entering MLs, of whom between 20 and 40 percent were SLIFE. Since the inception of this model, we have seen a steady increase in standardized test scores and the number of SLIFE meeting graduation requirements.

In this chapter, we provide an overview of our spiraling approach to instruction, designed to meet the needs of SLIFE and other struggling MLs at the forefront. Our model is based on Bruner's (1960) concept of spiral curriculum. Bruner advanced the idea that even the most complex ideas can be taught to all children, regardless of their stage of development, as long as those ideas are introduced first at a simplified level and are then revisited later at a more complex level. As Bruner (1960) notes, "We begin with the hypothesis that any subject can be taught in some intellectually honest form to any child at any stage of development" (p. 30). According to this vision, concepts and skills are revisited periodically, each time at a level of gradually increasing difficulty. Although Bruner predicated the spiral curriculum model on cognitive development, we interpreted his work through the lens of second language acquisition. If anything can be taught to anyone, we thought, then why not the highest-order thinking skills to students at the lowest levels of English proficiency? And thus, the idea of the spiraling curriculum for newcomer MLs and SLIFE was born.

The spiraling curriculum model focuses on revisiting key language skills multiple times throughout the year—a significant departure from traditional instructional approaches that go from basic to more complex skills as the school year progresses. The model's approach addresses the issue of ongoing enrollment by leveling the playing field for new students and challenging current students to delve deeper into certain topics (Wright, 2015; Zwiers & Crawford, 2011). Aligned to the CCSS, our model focuses on content-rich nonfiction, citing textual evidence to support claims, and interacting with peers using complex academic discourse. You will see in this chapter how the strategies presented in this book are woven together and revisited, providing the support and consistency our students need while also challenging them by keeping rigor and expectations high.

We came to the realization that a spiraling model was needed when discussing our traditional ELD scope and sequence with content-area teachers. Many years ago, we would introduce the past tense around January—prompting our history colleagues to half-jokingly remark, "Great! So this means that our students will finally be able to start understanding our content in January?" Jokes aside, they brought up a very valid concern. Why *were* we waiting so long to teach such an essential language skill? This forced us to take a hard look at our scope and sequence.

We knew we needed to revise what we were doing in order to give students a real chance to access instruction in all their content areas. In our new approach, students review past tense (among other verb tenses) a minimum of four times throughout the school year. Each time, they delve deeper into the topic. We use this same spiraling strategy to teach a variety of language skills, including comparing and contrasting, presenting information, citing textual evidence, and so on.

FIGURE 4.1

Spiraling Curriculum Model

Spiraling Curriculum			
Unit 1: Identity	**Unit 2: Inspiration**	**Unit 3: Impact**	**Unit 4: Initiative**
Language Skills			
• Compare and contrast • Sequence events • Justify an opinion • Cite textual evidence • Write an open response • Analyze a text • Present information	Identify, recognize, and use: • Simple verb tenses • Progressive verb tenses • Modal verbs • Singular and plural nouns • Descriptive adjectives, comparatives, and superlatives		Identify, recognize, and pronounce: • Single consonants • Consonant blends and digraphs • Long and short vowels • Vowel digraphs • Homonyms, homophones, and homographs
Essential Questions • Who are we? What defines us? • What shapes our identities? • How does our personal journey influence who we are?	**Essential Questions** • What makes a role model? • How do role models inspire us to be better? • How do challenges and achievements shape our lives?	**Essential Questions** • How is our world evolving? • What is the impact of change? • How do our experiences influence our perspectives?	**Essential Questions** • How can we make responsible decisions? • How can we use language effectively and clearly in order to solve problems? • How can we take initiative to improve ourselves, our communities, and our world?

Vocabulary	Vocabulary	Vocabulary	Vocabulary
• Identify • Explain • Analyze • Compare and contrast • Inference • Evidence	• Sequence • Research • Paraphrase • Annotate • Describe • Develop	• Persuade • Justify • Cause and effect • Debate • Support • Evaluate	• Contribute • Initiate • Predict • Elaborate • Examine • Apply
SEL Focus	**SEL Focus**	**SEL Focus**	**SEL Focus**
• Identifying emotions • Accurate self-image • Recognizing assets • Confidence • Self-efficacy • Setting goals	• Self-control • Managing stress • Building self-discipline • Motivation • Organizational skills • Teamwork	• Perspective taking • Empathy • Appreciating diversity • Respecting others • Evaluating • Reflecting	• Problem solving • Analyzing situations • Taking responsibility • Community participation

Note: Content in the SEL Focus row adapted from the CASEL (2017, 2020) Framework.

Understanding and Using Our Model

Our spiraling curriculum model is broken down into four major units, one for each quarter of the school year. The major unit themes are identity, inspiration, impact, and initiative. In line with the SIOP Model, the CCSS, and culturally responsive teaching methods, this model provides educators with ample opportunity to assess students in ways that are "informal, authentic, and multidimensional, with multiple indicators" to demonstrate proficiency (Echevarría et al., 2014, pp. 212–213). Each unit includes a culminating project inspired by the Understanding by Design framework (Wiggins & McTighe, 2005), Hess's cognitive rigor matrices (Hess, 2004, 2005), and project-based learning (PBL) principles (see Figure 4.2 for examples).

Whenever we talk to educators about our spiraling curriculum model, they often respond with "So, wait, you are teaching the same thing four times?" We always remind them that it is the language skills that

Figure 4.2

Sample Culminating Assessments

Unit 1: Identity
Content Topic: Personal Journey
Language Skills: compare and contrast; justify an opinion; cite textual evidence, present information; analyze a text; simple present tense; simple past tense; simple future tense

Assessment
• **Listening and Speaking:** Create a digital story about your immigration experience using a program of your choice. Present your digital story to class and answer questions from the audience.
• **Reading:** Read immigration stories and answer text-dependent questions.
• **Writing:** Write two or three paragraphs in response to the prompt below.
• **Prompt:** Describe your immigration experience. How did you get here? How did you feel about the immigration process? Why did you immigrate? What challenges did you overcome? How did these challenges help you to recognize your own strengths? How is your life now compared with your life in your native country? What are your goals here? Use specific reasons and textual evidence (from immigration stories and graphs) to support your ideas.

Unit 2: Inspiration
Content Topic: Inspirational People
Language Skills: compare and contrast; justify an opinion; cite textual evidence, present information; analyze a text; simple present tense; simple past tense; simple future tense

Assessment
• **Listening and Speaking:** In pairs or small groups, research an inspirational person of your choice. Each team member will present their research to class and answer questions from the audience.
• **Reading:** Independently and in small groups, read and analyze a biography of an inspirational person of your choice and answer text-dependent questions.
• **Writing:** Write five paragraphs in response to the prompt below.
• **Prompt:** Research an inspirational person. What were their challenges? What were their achievements? Why are they inspirational to you? How do they motivate you to overcome challenges in your own life? Use specific reasons and textual evidence to support your ideas.

Unit 3: Impact
Content Topic: Impact of Technology
Language Skills: compare and contrast; justify an opinion; cite textual evidence, present information; analyze a text; simple present tense; simple past tense; simple future tense

Assessment
• **Listening and Speaking:** Debate the issue of whether technology is making our lives better or worse with your classmates. Describe the advantages or disadvantages of technology. Support your opinion with textual evidence and personal experiences. Agree and disagree respectfully with your peers.
• **Reading:** Read and analyze an informational text about technology and the impact it has on our lives. Answer text-dependent questions.
• **Writing:** Using a graphic organizer, write a three- to four-paragraph essay in response to the prompt.
• **Prompt:** Is technology making our lives better or worse? What are the advantages and disadvantages of technology? Justify your opinion with examples from the text.

Unit 4: Initiative
Content Topic: Environmental Issues
Language Skills: compare and contrast; justify an opinion; cite textual evidence, present information; analyze a text; simple present tense; simple past tense; simple future tense

Assessment
• **Listening and Speaking:** Participate in a Socratic seminar on the environmental issue of disappearing honeybees. Respond to discussion questions from the point of view of one of the following community member groups: farmers, beekeepers, Congress members, biologists, and concerned citizens.
• **Reading:** Read informational texts and answer text-dependent questions.
• **Writing:** Write three or four paragraphs in response to the prompt below.
• **Prompt:** Write a letter to an elected official explaining the causes and effects of the honeybee's decline. Be sure to cite evidence from the text (informational text, research, graphs) to support your claims. From the perspective of your community group, explain your priorities and concerns. Include a new idea or regulation that would help solve this problem.

---

are "spiraled" or revisited, not the topics, texts, vocabulary, and so on. As you can see in Figure 4.1, these language skills (e.g., analyzing an informational text, writing an open response, and giving a presentation) are integrated into all four units. Consequently, students can revisit and delve deeper into each language skill each time, with a minimum of four opportunities throughout the year. This contrasts sharply with a traditional curriculum approach that becomes progressively more complex, widening the achievement gap between struggling MLs and their mainstream counterparts.

To illustrate, take a look at Figure 4.2, which shows four examples of culminating assessments designed for an ELD 1 SLIFE self-contained class. The language skills assessed through all four units are the same, but the text, content topic, and prompts differ. This allows all students to build competence, fluency, and confidence each time they revisit each language skill.

As Figure 4.2 shows, in Unit 1, students are tasked with reading and analyzing stories about the immigration journeys of others. They are then asked to create a personal narrative and digital storytelling video that details their own immigration experience and compares and contrasts their life now with life in their native country. Unit 2 asks students to research an inspirational person of their choice and write an essay focused on this individual's challenges and achievements by using textual evidence in support of their claims. In Unit 3, students are supposed to write an open-response essay about the advantages and disadvantages of technology and to justify their claims with textual evidence. The same skills (writing an open response, justifying claims with textual evidence) are emphasized in the culminating assessment for Unit 4, which prompts students to write a letter to an elected official explaining the causes and effects of the honeybee's decline as well as supporting their solution for solving this problem with evidence from various sources.

To illustrate the importance of the spiraling model, consider, for a moment, that it is the middle of the school year and you have just enrolled in a new school in a country whose language you don't speak. Half of the skills you need to acquire and demonstrate proficiency in have already been taught. Given the option of waiting until the start of the next school year to learn these skills that you have missed or beginning right away, in the second half of the current year, what choice would you make? We think we know the answer.

SEL Connection

If you closely examine Figure 4.2, you will see that we designed our culminating assessments with an SEL focus in mind. Unit 1 focuses on identifying emotions and goal setting, Unit 2 on self-motivation and reflecting, Unit 3 on evaluating and respect for others, and Unit 4 on perspective taking and solving problems.

Throughout the process of integrating SEL competencies into curriculum and instruction, we found that at times educators, ourselves included, tend to navigate toward the competencies that are "easiest" to align with our content. Although "communication" and "respect for others" are undoubtedly important, we would like to challenge you to expand your horizons. As you become better acquainted with the strategies in this book, we encourage you to seek ways to integrate a broad range of SEL competencies into your culminating assessments. Ask yourself, *What does self-efficacy look like in a content-specific assessment for MLs? How can the SEL competency of impulse control be integrated into our culminating project?* We encourage you to keep a laminated copy of CASEL's SEL competencies (2020) by your side as you are planning and posted in your classroom, as we do!

Now It's Your Turn: Questions and Exercises

- What are some drawbacks of a traditional, strictly linear approach to curriculum? How does such an approach affect schools with challenges related to ongoing enrollment?
- How can a spiraling curriculum model serve the needs of SLIFE and struggling MLs? What are some advantages and disadvantages of implementing such a model?
- Use the spiraling curriculum model presented in this chapter as a guide to formulate language skills, essential questions, vocabulary, and SEL competencies that would address the needs of your learners. Discuss the rationale for focusing on these aspects.

5

Putting It All Together:
A Spiraling Curriculum Unit

In this chapter, we present the various strategies introduced so far within the context of a complete unit plan. Our hope is that you will see how the strategies come together to optimize learning, like pieces of a puzzle forming a bigger picture. Although the unit plan in this chapter was designed for a self-contained SLIFE class, the overall concept is applicable in any classroom where SLIFE and struggling MLs are enrolled.

The summative assessments for the unit in this chapter include a debate on the impact of technology and an essay evaluating its advantages and disadvantages. The unit plan is aligned to the SIOP Model (Echevarría et al., 2004) as well as to higher-order thinking skills identified by Bloom (1956) and Webb (1997). As you read through the plan, notice how the unit vocabulary (*persuade, justify, cause and effect, debate, support, evaluate*) is embedded through various prompts and scaffolding tools. The unit is also aligned to the CCSS.

We were inspired to develop the unit by the Understanding by Design framework (Wiggins & McTighe, 2005), project-based learning principles, Hess's cognitive rigor matrices (Hess, 2004, 2005; Hess et al., 2009), and the SIOP Model (Echevarría et al., 2004). In keeping with SIOP Model recommendations, our lessons include content and language objectives, content concepts that are appropriate for the age and educational background of our students, the use of high-quality supplementary materials, adapted content, and meaningful activities that integrate all four language domains. Each lesson includes a language and content objective, SEL connections, and an agenda of lesson activities and assessments.

Pay close attention to the SEL competencies with which this unit aligns: perspective taking, empathy, appreciating diversity, respecting others, evaluating, and reflecting. We've integrated these competencies organically throughout the unit, from having students evaluate and reflect on various perspectives during text analysis to requiring them to respectfully express their point of view during a debate. Infusing SEL into instruction is especially important for SLIFE and struggling MLs, since social-emotional well-being significantly influences the process of language acquisition (Brown, 2007).

Our approach to integrating SEL into instruction is based on the premise that "learning is social, emotional, and academic" (Darling-Hammond & Cook-Harvey, 2018). To help our students engage at a deeper level with the SEL competencies, we have integrated them in a spiraling fashion, enabling new students to gain exposure to the competencies while allowing students already enrolled in the program to revisit the competencies in a different context.

The accessible text at the center of our unit plan is shown in Figure 5.1. Accessible texts include "authentic adapted texts, modified in terms of lexical density, syntactic complexity, and length (Bowers et al., 2010), or highly engaging, easily comprehensible texts (e.g., Chamot et al., 2013)" (Filimon, 2023). The unit plan itself is shown in Figure 5.2.

Following is a comprehensive outline of each of the lessons in our technology unit, including time frame, implementation steps, aligned standards, and specific lesson activities.

FIGURE 5.1

Is Technology Making Our Lives Better or Worse?

 **Technology** impacts our lives every day. When we use our cell phones, drive our cars, or get on our computers, we are using technology. However, whether technology is making our lives better or worse is a **controversial** issue.

Many people are **excited** about using technology because they think it makes everyday activities faster. For example, instead of writing and mailing a letter, people can send an email from their computers. Also, they can now use cell phones to communicate with their friends and family, even if they live far away. In addition, they can get to work or school easily by driving a car or taking a bus.

Other people are **concerned** about the use of technology because they think it can be **distracting** and even **dangerous**. They say that many accidents happen because people are distracted by their cell phones while driving. Also, they **worry** about how much time people spend using their cell phones and computers, instead of talking to their friends in person. Finally, they believe that instead of **relying on** cars or buses to go short  distances, people should walk or ride a bike because this is better for their health and the environment.

What do you think?
Be ready to **justify** your **opinion**!

Figure 5.2

Technology Unit Plan

Unit Title: The Impact of Technology		Length of Unit: 3–4 weeks	
Unit Goals	• Explain by describing opposing points of view supported with relevant details and evidence. • Argue by stating points and counterpoints supported with reasoning and evidence.	**Essential Questions**	• How is our world evolving? • What is the impact of change? • How do our experiences influence our perspectives?
Unit Guiding Questions	• What are the impacts of technology on your life and the world around you? • How does your experience with technology shape your perspective? What can you learn from the perspectives of others? • How can we use language effectively and clearly to influence others?		
Language Skills	• Compare and contrast • Sequence events • Justify an opinion • Cite textual evidence • Write an open response • Analyze a text • Present information	**Cross-curricular Vocabulary**	• *Persuade* • *Justify* • *Cause and effect* • *Debate* • *Support* • *Evaluate*
Hess's Cognitive Rigor Matrix	**DOK 3: Strategic Thinking or Reasoning:** Support an opinion, argument, or disagreement with evidence, reasoning. **DOK 4: Extended Thinking:** Research a topic with evidence pro-con for debate, essay, or cartoon; research and present performance or presentation using multiple sources.	**Target CASEL SEL Competencies**	**Social Awareness** • Perspective-taking • Empathy • Appreciating diversity • Respect for others **Responsible Decision Making** • Evaluating • Reflecting
Unit Standards			
WIDA English Language Development (ELD) Standards	• **English Language Development Standard 1:** English language learners communicate for Social and Instructional purposes within the school setting. • **English Language Development Standard 2:** English language learners communicate information, ideas, and concepts necessary for academic success in the content area of Language Arts.		

(continued)

FIGURE 5.2—(*continued*)
Technology Unit Plan

Unit Standards—(*continued*)	
Common Core State Standards	
Speaking and Listening	• **CCSS.ELA-LITERACY.SL.9-10.1.B:** Work with peers to set rules for collegial discussions and decision-making (e.g., informal consensus, taking votes on key issues, presentation of alternate views), clear goals and deadlines, and individual roles as needed. • **CCSS.ELA-LITERACY.SL.9-10.3:** Evaluate a speaker's point of view, reasoning, and use of evidence and rhetoric, identifying any fallacious reasoning or exaggerated or distorted evidence. • **CCSS.ELA-LITERACY.SL.9-10.4:** Present information, findings, and supporting evidence clearly, concisely, and logically such that listeners can follow the line of reasoning and the organization, development, substance, and style are appropriate to purpose, audience, and task. • **CCSS.ELA-LITERACY.SL.9-10.5:** Make strategic use of digital media (e.g., textual, graphical, audio, visual, and interactive elements) in presentations to enhance understanding of findings, reasoning, and evidence and to add interest.
Reading	• **CCSS.ELA-LITERACY.RI.9-10.1:** Cite strong and thorough textual evidence to support analysis of what the text says explicitly as well as inferences drawn from the text. • **CCSS.ELA-LITERACY.RI.9-10.3:** Analyze how the author unfolds an analysis or series of ideas or events, including the order in which the points are made, how they are introduced and developed, and the connections that are drawn between them.
Writing	• **CCSS.ELA-LITERACY.W.9-10.2:** Write informative/explanatory texts to examine and convey complex ideas, concepts, and information clearly and accurately through the effective selection, organization, and analysis of content. • **CCSS.ELA-LITERACY.W.9-10.2.B:** Develop the topic with well-chosen, relevant, and sufficient facts, extended definitions, concrete details, quotations, or other information and examples appropriate to the audience's knowledge of the topic. • **CCSS.ELA-LITERACY.W.9-10.7:** Conduct short as well as more sustained research projects to answer a question (including a self-generated question) or solve a problem; narrow or broaden the inquiry when appropriate; synthesize multiple sources on the subject, demonstrating understanding of the subject under investigation.
Language	• **CCSS.ELA-LITERACY.L.9-10.1:** Demonstrate command of the conventions of standard English grammar and usage when writing or speaking. • **CCSS.ELA-LITERACY.L.9-10.6:** Acquire and use accurately general academic and domain-specific words and phrases, sufficient for reading, writing, speaking, and listening at the college and career readiness level; demonstrate independence in gathering vocabulary knowledge when considering a word or phrase important to comprehension or expression.

In this unit, students will develop academic language, including:
• Content and topic-specific vocabulary (e.g., *technology, impact, advantages, disadvantages*).   • Simple present tense structure (interrogative, negative and positive).   • Comparative adjectives related to the topic (e.g., *better, worse, faster, slower*).   • Argument language for stating opinions and supporting them with evidence (e.g., *I believe, I agree/disagree, according to the text, the author states*).   • Transition words to sequence ideas (e.g., *first, next, finally*).   • Structure of short explanatory paragraphs composed of multiple sentences that incorporate transition words.   • Characteristics of effective presentations (e.g., clear pronunciation, eye contact, language control, use of supporting visuals).

In this unit, students will develop various language skills, including the ability to:
• Use content and topic-specific vocabulary to analyze multiple points of view (e.g., *technology, impact, advantages, disadvantages*).   • Discuss and write opinions using comparative adjectives (e.g., *better, worse, faster, slower*).   • Summarize research findings using present tense verbs.   • State an opinion, orally and in writing, and support it with relevant details and evidence.   • Use transition words (e.g., *first, next, finally*) to introduce ideas.   • Make points and counterpoints in a debate using argument language (e.g., *I believe, I agree, I disagree*).   • Communicate research findings using appropriate presentation skills (e.g., clear pronunciation, eye contact, language control, and use of supporting visuals).

Assessments	
Criteria	Teachers will assess students' ability to demonstrate: • Appropriate use of content and topic-related vocabulary (e.g., *technology, impact, advantages, disadvantages*). • Accurate use of verbs in simple present to summarize research findings. • Appropriate use of comparative adjectives (e.g., *better, worse, faster, slower*) to discuss and write opinions. • Effective use of transition words (e.g., *first, next, finally*) to introduce ideas. • Appropriate use of sentence frames to justify opinions with textual evidence (e.g., *according to the text, the author states*). • Effective application of oral presentation skills (e.g., clear pronunciation, eye contact, language control, use of supporting visuals). • Effective use of argument language to make points and counterpoints in a debate (e.g., *I believe, I agree, I disagree*).
Formative Assessments	• Do-now activities • Exit tickets • Turn-and-talk • Graphic organizers • Color-coded model responses

(continued)

FIGURE 5.2—*(continued)*
Technology Unit Plan

Assessments—*(continued)*		
Summative Assessments	The following is the end-of-unit culminating project, distinguished by language domain:	
	Listening and Speaking	**Reading**
	Is technology making our lives better or worse? Debate this issue by respectfully agreeing and disagreeing with your peers.	Conduct research on the advantages and disadvantages of a technological device and the impact it has on our lives by reading short informational texts. Organize your research findings and present them using a poster or a digital presentation program of your choice.
	Writing	
	Essay: How do various technological devices impact our lives? Explain the advantages and disadvantages of one technological device. Justify your opinion with specific examples and textual evidence.	

Lesson 1: Building Background

Lesson at a Glance: In today's class, you will introduce your students to a new unit about technology by engaging with key content. Students will learn topic vocabulary and form sentences with vocabulary words to describe how technology is used on a daily basis. In addition, students will strengthen their pronunciation by practicing the consonant digraphs *sh*, *th*, and *ph*, which they encounter in many of the words in the text.

Time Frame: one 75-minute period

Materials

- Turn-and-talk template (Figure 1.2)
- Vocabulary turn-and-talk template (Figure 2.1)
- Graphic organizer based on the Frayer model (Figure 2.2)
- Consonant digraphs practice worksheet (Figure 5.3)
- Impacts of technology vocabulary cloze activity (Figure 5.4)
- *Optional:* Computer/projector
- *Optional:* Student notebooks or binders
- *Optional:* Videos and images about the advantages and disadvantages of technology
- *Optional:* Pocket chart and index cards for consonant digraphs

Preparation

1. Display the following objectives and SEL focus on a whiteboard, chart paper, or slide presentation:
   - **Content Objective:** Analyze the positive and negative impacts of technology on daily life.
   - **Language Objective:** Discuss how technology affects daily life using content vocabulary words (*technology, impact, advantages, disadvantages*).
   - **SEL Focus:** Evaluating

- **CCSS Standard:** CCSS.ELA-LITERACY.L.9-10.6: Acquire and use accurately general academic and domain-specific words and phrases, sufficient for reading, writing, speaking, and listening at the college and career readiness level; demonstrate independence in gathering vocabulary knowledge when considering a word or phrase important to comprehension or expression.

2. Create your agenda using the following lesson activities.
3. Prepare the necessary materials.
4. Prepare a word wall for the content vocabulary words (*technology, impact, advantages, disadvantages*) and other unit words (e.g., *health, should*). Include native language support where necessary.
5. Ensure seating arrangements enable peer-to-peer discussion.

Activities

1. *Do-now activity:* Use the turn-and-talk template to build background knowledge about how students use technology at home and at school. Have the students answer the first two questions and then model the procedure with the help of a student. Provide pictures if desired. Allow students to write their answers first, if desired. Circulate to help students, as needed.
2. Discuss the content objective, language objective, and SEL focus with students.
3. Explain how the unit will begin by introducing important vocabulary and reviewing ways to use language to discuss an important topic (e.g., "We will begin by learning some new words that we will use in the course of the unit").
4. Preteach key content vocabulary words: *technology, controversial, impact, advantage, disadvantage.*
5. Use the vocabulary turn-and-talk template and the graphic organizer based on the Frayer model to introduce and discuss each word.
6. Provide each student with a hard copy of the graphic organizer for each vocabulary word to use during the lesson.

7. After preteaching vocabulary words, return to the turn-and-talk template from the beginning of the lesson. Encourage students to complete questions 3–5 about the positive and negative impacts of technology.

8. When students are ready, have them engage in the slide-and-glide strategy from Chapter 2 (see p. 54) to build background knowledge and use new vocabulary words with their peers.

9. Introduce the consonant digraphs *th*, *sh*, and *ph*. If possible, post index cards with these digraphs and example words in a pocket chart at the front of the room. Explain to students that many of the words they will encounter in the unit (e.g., *health*, *should*, *short*, *phone*) contain these digraphs. Model the correct pronunciation and have the students repeat chorally.

10. Have students pair up to sort the words into columns on their consonant digraphs practice worksheet. Circulate and provide assistance, as necessary.

11. *Exit ticket:* Have students complete the impacts of technology vocabulary cloze activity (Figure 5.4) using the vocabulary words.

12. *Optional lesson extension activity:* Have students write four original sentences in their notebooks using the vocabulary words.

Assessment

- *Formative:* Assess students' ability to use content- and topic-specific vocabulary (e.g., *technology, impact, advantages, disadvantages*).
- *Formative:* Assess students' ability to work with peers following specific norms for discussion.

FIGURE 5.3

Consonant Digraphs Practice Worksheet

Name: _____   **Date:** _____

Consonant digraphs contain two consonants that make one sound. Here are some examples:

short   health   should   phone   shut   alphabet   paragraph   share   think

Sort these words into the correct column. Add more examples from texts that you have read.

sh	th	ph

FIGURE 5.4

Impacts of Technology Vocabulary Cloze Activity

Name: _____   **Date:** _____

Complete the paragraph with the words in the box.

technology   impact   advantage   disadvantage

   We are surrounded by many types of _____—for example, cell phones, computers, cars, and televisions. There are both positive and negative effects of technology. One _____ of technology is how easy and fast it is to use. One _____ of technology is how distracting it can be. One thing is for certain, technology has a major _____ on our lives!

Lesson 2: Reading and Analyzing an Informational Text

Lesson at a Glance: Students will read the text "Is Technology Making Our Lives Better or Worse?" (Figure 5.1) using a variety of reading strategies including echo reading, partner reading, and annotating. They will answer text-dependent questions orally and in writing. Vocabulary from Lesson 1 will be reinforced.

Time Frame: two 75-minute periods

Materials

- Red and green colored pencils or highlighters
- Reading comprehension template (Figure 2.3)
- True/false–evidence from text template (Figure 2.7)
- "Is Technology Making Our Lives Better or Worse?" text (Figure 5.1)
- T-notes graphic organizer (Figure 1.9)
- Sticky notes
- *Optional:* Computer/projector
- *Optional:* Student notebooks or binders

Preparation

1. Display the following objectives and SEL focus on a whiteboard, chart paper, or slide presentation:
   - **Content Objective:** Read and analyze an informational text.
   - **Language Objective:** Answer text-dependent questions using the reading comprehension template.
   - **SEL Focus:** Analyzing situations
   - **CCSS Standard:** CCSS.ELA-LITERACY.RI.9-10.3: Analyze how the author unfolds an analysis or series of ideas or events, including the order in which the points are made, how they are introduced and developed, and the connections that are drawn between them.

2. Create your agenda using the following lesson activities.

3. Prepare the necessary materials.

4. Ensure seating arrangements enable peer-to-peer discussion.

Activities

1. *Do-now activity:* Engage students in a dictation activity to reinforce the previous lesson. Read each of the following words out aloud three times and have students write them in their notebooks: *health, phone, should, paragraph,* and *think.* Elicit volunteers to write each word on the board. Address any misconceptions about the consonant digraphs from Lesson 1 if needed.

2. Discuss the content objective, language objective, and SEL focus with students.

3. Preview the text by analyzing the title and pictures and making predictions.

4. Model reading: Read the text aloud to students while they follow along.

5. Echo reading: Engage the full class in an echo reading of the text. Pause after short phrases or sentences to allow students to repeat what they just heard in order to develop their pronunciation.

6. Partner reading: Have students pair up and complete the reading comprehension template, annotating key vocabulary using synonyms, cognates, and images, as needed.

7. Explain to students that they will use red and green colors to represent advantages and disadvantages within the text. Model this by using green to highlight one advantage. Have students highlight the remaining examples in pairs. Repeat this process using red to highlight one disadvantage. Have students work in pairs to find remaining examples. Have students share out and clarify any misconceptions as needed. Record the advantages and disadvantages that students shared using the T-notes graphic organizer.

8. *Exit ticket:* Ask students to list three advantages and three disadvantages of technology on a sticky note.

9. *Optional lesson extension activity:* Students brainstorm and list three advantages and three disadvantages related to the following topics (or to another of their choice): fast food; having a pet; living in the city; living in the countryside; school uniforms; school lunches.

Assessment

- *Formative:* Assess students' ability to use details from the text to support their textual analysis.
- *Formative:* Assess students' ability to apply learned language to discussing advantages and disadvantages of technology.

Lesson 3: Citing Textual Evidence

Lesson at a Glance: Students will read statements and determine whether they are true or false using the true/false–evidence from text template. Students will share out orally or using nonlinguistic demonstration of higher-order thinking.

Time Frame: one 75-minute period

Materials

- "Is Technology Making Our Lives Better or Worse?" text (Figure 5.1)
- Identifying advantages and disadvantages chart (Figure 5.5)
- True/false–evidence from text template (Figure 2.7)
- *Optional:* True/false–evidence from text (additional practice) template (Figure 5.6)

Preparation

1. Display the following objectives and SEL focus on a whiteboard, chart paper, or slide presentation:
   - **Content Objective:** Read and analyze an informational text.
   - **Language Objective:** Evaluate true and false statements about the text using textual evidence.
   - **SEL Focus:** Evaluating
   - **CCSS Standard:** CCSS.ELA-LITERACY.RI.9-10.1: Cite strong and thorough textual evidence to support analysis of what the text says explicitly as well as inferences drawn from the text.
2. Create your agenda using the following lesson activities.
3. Prepare the necessary materials.
4. Ensure seating arrangements enable pair or group work.

Activities

1. *Do-now activity:* Have students identify advantages and disadvantages of technology using the identifying advantages and disadvantages chart.

2. Discuss the content objective, language objective, and SEL focus with students.

3. Hand out copies of the true/false–evidence from text template. Explain to students that they will read and evaluate statements from the text and determine if the statements are true or false. Model this by answering the first question as a think-aloud. Then elicit students' help with the second question. Encourage students to show their evidence orally or using nonlinguistic demonstrations of critical thinking (e.g., by pointing or underlining the section of text that proves the statement true or false). Model using this sentence stem to prepare students for a subsequent lesson: "This is [true/false] because the text says, '_____.'"

4. Allow students to work in pairs if desired. Circulate and help students as they continue to evaluate the true/false statements.

5. Write *true* and *false* on pieces of paper and post them at different ends of the room, or write the words on opposite ends of the board. Read the last two statements and have students stand up and move to the side of the room accordingly. Call on students to share their evidence.

6. *Exit ticket:* Have students create their own true/false statement on a sticky note. Ask students to challenge their partner orally to determine if the statement is true or false.

7. *Optional lesson extension activity:* Have students complete the true/false–evidence from text (additional practice) template.

Assessment

- *Formative:* Assess students' ability to cite textual evidence in support of their reasoning.
- *Formative:* Assess students' ability to evaluate text-based claims.

FIGURE 5.5

Identifying Advantages and Disadvantages Chart

Name: _____ **Date:** _____

Identify whether the statement reflects an advantage or disadvantage by writing *A* or *D* in the left column.

Advantage or Disadvantage?	Statement
	1. Technology makes everyday activities faster. For example, instead of writing and mailing a letter, people can send an email from their computers.
	2. Technology can be distracting and even dangerous.
	3. Many accidents happen because people are distracted by their cell phones while driving.
	4. We can use cell phones to communicate with friends and family, even if they live far away.

FIGURE 5.6

True/False–Evidence from Text (Additional Practice) Template

Statement	True/False–Evidence from Text
1. All people are excited about technology.	This is _____ because the text says, _____ _____ _____
2. People can get to work easily by taking a bus or car.	This is _____ because the text says, _____ _____ _____
3. Taking a bus or car to work is good for our health and the environment.	This is _____ because the text says, _____ _____ _____

Lesson 4: Learning about Comparatives

Lesson at a Glance: Students will learn about comparative adjectives (e.g., *better, worse, faster, slower*) by identifying them in the text and using them in original sentences. Students will use what they learn in this lesson to describe technology throughout the unit in presentations, compositions, and debate.

Time Frame: two 75-minute periods

Materials

- Comparative images of technological devices (e.g., a fast car and a slow car, an old desktop computer and a new laptop, a black-and-white television and a flat-screen television)
- Chart paper
- Markers
- "Is Technology Making Our Lives Better or Worse?" text (Figure 5.1)
- Comparatives guided notes (Figure 5.7)
- Comparative forms activity (Figure 5.8)

Preparation

1. Display the following objectives and SEL focus on a whiteboard, chart paper, or slide presentation:
   - **Content Objective:** Compare advantages and disadvantages of technology.
   - **Language Objective:** Discuss and write opinions about advantages and disadvantages of technology using comparative adjectives (e.g., *better, worse, faster, slower*).
   - **SEL Focus:** Communication
   - **CCSS Standard:** CCSS.ELA-LITERACY.L.9-10.1: Demonstrate command of the conventions of standard English grammar and usage when writing or speaking.

2. Prepare the necessary materials. Depending on the levels of English proficiency in your class, you can prepare adapted versions of resources, such as Newsela.com articles on the negative and positive effects of technology, as well as videos on this topic.

3. Create your agenda using the following lesson activities.

4. Ensure seating arrangements enable pair or group work.

Activities

1. *Do-now activity:* Show students the comparative images of two technological devices (e.g., a fast car vs. a slow car; an old computer vs. a new laptop; a black-and-white television vs. a flat-screen television). Label the images A and B. Ask students to write observations using these sentence stems:
   - I can see _____.
   - I observe _____.
   - I notice _____.

2. After students create sentences, have them do a turn-and-talk with their partner using the question "What can you see in these pictures?" Elicit responses from students. On the board, keep a running list of any adjectives students use.

3. Discuss the content objective, language objective, and SEL focus with students.

4. Explain to students that they will be describing technology and its advantages and disadvantages using adjectives. Tell students that when we make comparisons between two things using adjectives, we call them *comparatives*. Use the adjectives that you collected from students to write some basic comparative sentences on the board. Here are some examples:
   - Television A is older than Television B.
   - Car A is faster than Car B.
   - Computer A is bigger than Computer B.
   - Car B is slower than Car A.

5. Refer back to the "Is Technology Making Our Lives Better or Worse?" text. Call students' attention to the comparatives within the title of the text. Use native language support if needed.

6. Use the comparatives guided notes to provide students with a mini-lesson on comparatives. Focus on high-frequency adjectives related to technology such as *better, worse, faster, slower, easier, harder, more/less distracting*, and *more/less dangerous*. Explain that if an adjective has one or two syllables, they should add *-er* to make it comparative (e.g., *faster*), and if it has more than two syllables, they should use *more* or *less* plus the adjective (e.g., *more dangerous*). Explain as well that *than* is used when making comparisons. Provide examples of sentences, and engage students in creating their own examples using the words provided.

7. Conduct a gallery walk activity using the images of technological items from the first activity. Put each pair of compared images on chart paper, and give students time to write a sentence on each using markers. Circulate around the room to help students, as needed.

8. *Exit ticket:* Have students complete the comparative forms activity.

9. *Optional lesson extension activity:* Write five original sentences using the following comparatives: *better than, worse than, faster than, slower than*, and *more dangerous than*.

Assessment

- *Formative:* Assess students' ability to apply learned language when making observations and describing images.
- *Formative:* Assess students' ability to use comparative adjectives to describe technology and its advantages and disadvantages.
- *Formative:* Assess students' ability to create original sentences using comparative adjectives.

FIGURE 5.7

Comparatives Guided Notes

Name: _____   **Date:** _____

One-Syllable Adjectives	Comparative Form
fast	faster than
_____	_____
_____	_____

Two-Syllable Adjectives	Comparative Form
easy	easier than
_____	_____
_____	_____

Adjectives with Three or More Syllables	Comparative Form
dangerous	more dangerous than less dangerous than
_____	_____
_____	_____

Adjectives with Irregular Comparative Forms	
Adjectives	Comparative Form
good	better than
_____	_____
_____	_____

Example Sentences Using Comparatives:

1. _____

2. _____

3. _____

4. _____

5. _____

FIGURE 5.8

Comparative Forms Activity

Name: _____   **Date:** _____

Circle the correct comparative form in the sentences below.

1. Cars and buses are **worse than / worst than** walking for our health and the environment.

2. Cars and buses are **more fast than / faster than** walking to school or work.

3. Writing a letter is **more slow than / slower than** sending an email.

Lesson 5: Learning About the Present Tense

Lesson at a Glance: Students will learn what the present tense is and how to form it, as well as the present-tense forms of common verbs such as *be, go, leave, eat, study*, and *do*. Students will identify the verbs used within the informational text "Is Technology Making Our Lives Better or Worse?" and will be able to give examples of signal words used with simple present tense (e.g., *every day, always, sometimes*). Students will use what they learn in this lesson to describe technology throughout the unit in various original products such as a presentation, a written composition, and a debate.

Time Frame: two 75-minute periods

Materials

- "Is Technology Making Our Lives Better or Worse?" text (Figure 5.1)
- Simple present tense guided notes (Figure 5.9)
- Class Q&A activity template (Figure 5.10)
- *Exit ticket:* Simple present tense activity (Figure 5.11)
- *Optional:* Clipboards

Preparation

1. Display the following objectives and SEL foci on a whiteboard, chart paper, or slide presentation:
   - **Content Objective:** Analyze routines and facts related to technology.
   - **Language Objective:** Describe and discuss routines and facts related to technology using verbs in the present tense.
   - **SEL Foci:** Teamwork, appreciating diversity, respect for others
   - **CCSS Standard:** CCSS.ELA-LITERACY.L.9-10.1: Demonstrate command of the conventions of standard English grammar and usage when writing or speaking.
2. Prepare the necessary materials.

3. Add high-frequency verbs to the word wall (e.g., *use, make, send, call, drive, have, go*).

4. Create your agenda using the following lesson activities.

5. Ensure seating arrangements enable pair or group work.

Activities

1. *Do-now activity:* Write the following question and answer frame on the board. Have students respond in writing. Ask a few students to share their answers with the whole class.

   How do you use technology every day?

   I use technology to _____.

2. Discuss the content objective, language objective, and SEL foci with students.

3. Explain to students that they will be using verbs to explain how they use technology and how technology affects their lives. Underline the verbs used in the do-now activity (e.g., "I use technology to call my friends"). If necessary, explain that a verb is the "action" in a sentence.

4. Practice identifying the verbs in the "Is Technology Making Our Lives Better or Worse?" text. First, model identifying and underlining verbs. Then encourage students to continue this process with a partner. Generate a list of verbs on the board. Have students write these verbs in their notebooks. Use native language support, if necessary.

5. Introduce the simple present tense to students. Consider showing a video about the simple present tense. Explain that the simple present tense is used for routines and facts. Provide examples of routines and facts (e.g., "I go to school every day," "This cell phone is black").

6. Have students complete the simple present tense guided notes. Explain that we add -s to verbs with the third-person singular (i.e., *he, she,* or *it*). Then complete the guided notes for three verbs from

the text. Follow the "I do, we do, you do" model by first modeling using the guided notes, then having students add to the document in pairs, and finally having students complete the work individually.

7. Model using the class Q&A activity template for students. Explain that they will ask questions to their classmates and write down their answers. Read the questions as a class. Use echo reading to practice pronunciation. Provide native language support, if needed.

8. Have students complete the class Q&A activity template by circulating around the room and asking the questions provided. If desired, provide students with clipboards.

9. *Exit ticket:* Have students complete the simple present tense activity.

10. *Optional lesson extension activity:* Have students write a paragraph about how the class uses technology using the responses from the class Q&A activity template.

Assessment

- *Formative:* Assess students' ability to discuss routines using simple present tense verbs appropriately.

- *Formative:* Assess students' ability to apply learned language when identifying and discussing simple present-tense verbs.

FIGURE 5.9

Simple Present Tense Guided Notes

Name: _____   **Date:** _____

Verb	Conjugation	Example Sentences
make	I make You make He makes She makes It makes We make They make	Technology makes our lives easier.

FIGURE 5.10

Class Q&A Activity Template

Name	Question	Response
	Do you think technology makes our life better or worse? How?	
	What type of technology do you use at school?	
	When do you use your cell phone?	
	Where do you use a computer?	
	What television shows do you like to watch?	

FIGURE 5.11

Simple Present Tense Activity

Name: _____ **Date:** _____

Circle the correct simple present tense verb.

1. Technology **make / makes** our life easier.

2. Sometimes people **have / has** accidents because of distracted driving.

3. We **talk / talks** to our friends face-to-face every day in class.

Lesson 6: Research Project

Lesson at a Glance: Students will create a poster or digital presentation detailing the advantages and disadvantages of a technological device of their choice (e.g., cars, cell phones, televisions).

Time Frame: three 75-minute periods

Materials

- Printed research resources or computers with internet access
- Research graphic organizer (Figure 5.12)
- *Optional:* Student notebooks or binders

Preparation

1. Display the following objectives and SEL foci on a whiteboard, chart paper, or slide presentation:
   - **Content Objective:** Create a poster or digital presentation on the advantages and disadvantages of a technological device.
   - **Language Objective:** Research the advantages and disadvantages of a technological device using a graphic organizer.
   - **SEL Foci:** Organizational skills, teamwork, reflection
   - **CCSS Standard:** CCSS.ELA-LITERACY.W.9-10.7: Conduct short as well as more sustained research projects to answer a question (including a self-generated question) or solve a problem; narrow or broaden the inquiry when appropriate; synthesize multiple sources on the subject, demonstrating understanding of the subject under investigation.
2. Prepare the necessary materials. Depending on the levels of English proficiency in your class, you can prepare adapted versions of resources, such as Newsela.com articles on the negative and positive effects of technology, as well as videos on this topic.
3. Create your agenda using the following lesson activities.
4. Ensure students have access to the internet and printed resources.
5. Ensure seating arrangements enable pair or group work.

Activities

1. *Do-now activity:* Write the following prompt on the board. Have students respond in writing. Have a few students share their answers with the whole class.

   List three of your favorite technological devices (e.g., computer, telephone, cell phone).

2. Discuss the content objective, language objective, and SEL foci.

3. Explain to students that they will research advantages and disadvantages of a chosen technological device using the research graphic organizer. Let students know that they will also present their research findings in a formal presentation and an essay.

4. Model one entry in the advantages section of the graphic organizer so students have a clear understanding of expectations. Next, explain to students that they need to cite their source in the research source(s) section. Address any questions they have.

5. With students' help, model one entry for the disadvantages and research source(s) (disadvantages) sections.

6. Explain to students that they will create a poster or digital presentation detailing their findings.

7. Provide a sample completed poster or digital presentation.

8. Give students ample time to work on their posters or digital presentation slides. Circulate and provide assistance, as necessary.

9. *Exit ticket:* Have students respond to the following prompt:

   What is one new fact you learned?

Assessment

- *Formative:* Assess students' ability to collect and organize information using a graphic organizer.
- *Summative:* Assess students' ability to create a poster/digital presentation based on their research findings.

FIGURE 5.12
Research Graphic Organizer

Advantages and Disadvantages of Technology

Names of Students	
Technological Device (e.g., computer, cell phone, television)	
Advantages	List three advantages of this technological device. 1. _____ 2. _____ 3. _____
Research Source(s) (Advantages)	List the source of your information for each advantage listed above. 1. _____ 2. _____ 3. _____
Disadvantages	List three disadvantages of this technological device. 1. _____ 2. _____ 3. _____
Research Source(s) (Disadvantages)	List the source of your information for each disadvantage listed above. 1. _____ 2. _____ 3. _____

Lesson 7: Presentations

Lesson at a Glance: Students will be able to apply their knowledge of vocabulary, comparatives, and simple present tense when presenting the advantages and disadvantages of a technological device.

Time Frame: one or two 75-minute periods (depending on class size)

Materials

- Presentation rubric (Figure 1.8)
- Sample presentation frames (Figure 1.4)
- Interactive note-taking template (Figure 1.5)
- Table tent for elaboration and clarification (Figure 1.7)

Preparation

1. Display the following objectives and SEL foci on a whiteboard, chart paper, or slide presentation:
   - **Content Objective:** Apply learned language when presenting the advantages and disadvantages of a technological item.
   - **Language Objective:** Present the advantages and disadvantages of a technological item using simple present verbs, comparatives, and target vocabulary: *advantages*, *disadvantages*, and *technological device*.
   - **SEL Foci:** Communication, appreciating diversity
   - **CCSS Standard:** CCSS.ELA-LITERACY.SL.9-10.4: Present information, findings, and supporting evidence clearly, concisely, and logically such that listeners can follow the line of reasoning and the organization, development, substance, and style are appropriate to purpose, audience, and task.
2. Prepare the necessary materials.
3. Create your agenda using the following lesson activities.
4. Create a sample poster or digital presentation to model appropriate presentation skills for students.

Activities

1. *Do-now activity:* Write the following information on the board. Have students assign a rating for each criteria in their notebooks, and select a few volunteers to share their explanations for assigning their ratings with the whole class.

    Rate the following characteristics of a good presentation on a scale of 1 to 3, with 1 being the most important and 3 being the least important:

    * Eye contact
    * Clarity
    * Pronunciation

2. Discuss the content objective, language objective, and SEL foci with students.

3. Go over the presentation rubric to familiarize students with the various criteria.

4. Introduce the sample presentation frames graphic organizer and model its use, if necessary, with an existing presentation.

5. Explain to students that in addition to paying attention to their peers' presentations, they will also have to take notes using the interactive note-taking template. Tell students that they can use the table tent for elaboration and clarification to help them fill out the template.

6. Model using the interactive note-taking template and the table tent for elaboration and clarification.

7. After each presentation, hold a two- to three-minute Q&A session to allow presenters to further demonstrate their knowledge of the topic and the students in the audience to fill out the interactive note-taking template. To ensure students in the audience participate equally in the Q&A, we recommend writing each of your students' names on craft sticks and putting them into a cup. After each presentation, draw a name from the cup and encourage that student to ask a question.

8. *Exit ticket:* Ask students to answer the following prompt:

What is one new thing that you learned today?

One new thing that I learned today is _____.

Assessment

- *Formative:* Assess students' application of learned language when presenting the advantages and disadvantages of a technological device.

- *Formative:* Assess students' ability to use comparative adjectives, simple present tense verbs, and target language (*advantages, disadvantages,* and *technological devices*) when presenting advantages and disadvantages.

- *Formative:* Assess students' ability to listen to an oral presentation and to ask and answer questions.

- *Summative:* Assess students' ability to communicate research findings using appropriate presentation skills (e.g., clear pronunciation, eye contact, language control, use of supporting visuals).

Lesson 8: Writing Protocol Overview

Lesson at a Glance: Students will be provided with an overview of the adapted writing with colors protocol. They will use colored pencils or highlighters to analyze and evaluate four compositions ranging in quality from exemplary to failing. They will identify strengths and areas for improvement before preparing to write their own compositions.

Time Frame: two or three 75-minute periods

Materials

- Citing textual evidence writing rubric (Figure 3.5)
- Adapted writing with colors charts: Teacher's guide and student's guide (Figure 3.3)
- Sample model responses #1 (Figure 3.1)
- Colored pencils or highlighters
- *Optional:* Computer/projector

Preparation

1. Display the following objectives and SEL focus on a whiteboard, chart paper, or slide presentation:
   - **Content Objective:** Analyze the characteristics of a well-developed explanatory essay.
   - **Language Objective:** Discuss the elements of a well-developed explanatory essay using academic vocabulary: *introduction, topic sentence, explanation, transition words, textual evidence,* and *conclusion.*
   - **SEL Focus:** Evaluating
   - **CCSS Standard:** CCSS.ELA-LITERACY.RI.9-10.3: Analyze how the author unfolds an analysis or series of ideas or events, including the order in which the points are made, how they are introduced and developed, and the connections that are drawn between them.

2. Prepare the necessary materials.

3. Create your agenda using the following lesson activities.

4. Ensure that the seating arrangement enables students to work in pairs.

Activities

1. *Do-now activity:* Have students rearrange the following sentences in the correct order so that the paragraph makes sense:
   - There are many advantages of technology.
   - Second, we can use cell phones to talk to our friends and family from different countries.
   - First, we can use computers to communicate faster.
   - According to the text, "Instead of writing and mailing a letter, people can send an email from their computers."

   When students finish, ask them to share out. Discuss the correct answer, as follows: "There are many advantages of technology. First, we can use computers to communicate faster. According to the text, 'Instead of writing and mailing a letter, people can send an email from their computers.' Second, we can use cell phones to talk to our friends and family from different countries."

2. Discuss the content objective, language objective, and SEL focus with students.

3. Go over the citing textual evidence writing rubric to familiarize students with the criteria that will be used to assess their writing.

4. Introduce the teacher's guide version of the adapted writing with colors chart, and explain to students that they are going to use colored pencils or highlighters to analyze the sample model responses #1 text: pink for the introduction, conclusion, and topic sentences; orange for transition words; blue for explanations; and green for quotations and other supporting textual evidence. Give students copies of the student's guide version of the chart and colored

pencils or highlighters. Have students color or highlight each field in the second column according to the color scheme.

5. Introduce the sample model responses #1. As a whole class, identify the introduction, the explanations, and the supporting evidence from the exemplary model response. Introduce the orange color for transition words (e.g., *first, second, in addition, finally*).

6. As a whole class, analyze the proficient model response to allow students more guided practice with color-coding.

7. Have students compare the exemplary and proficient sample responses and identify the differences between them.

8. In pairs, ask students to color-code the needs improvement and failing sample responses.

9. Conduct a whole-class discussion about the differences among the four sample responses revealed through the color-coding process.

10. Call students' attention to the lengthy failing sample response so they can see that the quality of a text is not necessarily determined by its length. If students do not notice on their own, bring to their attention that the failing model response is copied verbatim from the "Is Technology Making Our Lives Better or Worse?" text.

11. *Exit ticket:* Ask students to arrange the following transition words in the correct sequence: *finally, second, first.*

Assessment

- *Formative:* Assess students' ability to identify and discuss the elements of a well-developed explanatory essay (e.g., topic sentence, explanation, transition words, textual evidence).

Lesson 9: Writing a Composition

Lesson at a Glance: Students will have an opportunity to apply what they have learned about technology when writing about the advantages and disadvantages of a technological device and justifying their opinions.

Time Frame: two 75-minute periods

Materials

- Color-coding practice activity #1 (Figure 5.13)
- Citing textual evidence writing rubric (Figure 3.5)
- Claim-evidence graphic organizer (Figure 3.4)
- Color-coding practice activity #2 (Figure 5.14)
- Colored pencils or highlighters
- *Optional:* Computer/projector

Preparation

1. Display the following objectives and SEL foci on a whiteboard, chart paper, or slide presentation:
   - **Content Objective:** Create a composition about the advantages and disadvantages of a technological device.
   - **Language Objective:** Explain in writing the advantages and disadvantages of a technological device using a graphic organizer.
   - **SEL Foci:** Communication, organizational skills
   - **CCSS Standard:** CCSS.ELA-LITERACY.W.9-10.2: Write informative/explanatory texts to examine and convey complex ideas, concepts, and information clearly and accurately through the effective selection, organization, and analysis of content.
2. Prepare the necessary materials.
3. Create your agenda using the following lesson activities.
4. Ensure that the seating arrangement enables students to work in pairs.

Activities

1. *Do-now activity:* Distribute the color-coding practice activity #1 and ask students to complete it.

2. Discuss the content objective, language objective, and SEL foci with students.

3. Explain to students that in this lesson, they will apply what they have learned about academic writing by writing their own compositions explaining the advantages and disadvantages of the technological device that they researched in Lesson 6.

4. Go over the citing textual evidence writing rubric again to remind students of the criteria that will be used to assess their writing.

5. Go over the writing prompt:

   > How do various technological devices impact our lives? Explain the advantages and disadvantages of one technological device. Justify your opinion with specific examples and textual evidence.

6. Introduce the claim-evidence graphic organizer. Model completing the topic sentence and first explanation with students' help. If possible, use a projector so the whole class can see the process.

7. Have students complete the rest of the first body paragraph based on their own research. Circulate around the room and provide assistance, as necessary.

8. Introduce the second body paragraph. Model completing the topic sentence and first explanation with students' help. If possible, use a projector so the whole class can see the process.

9. Have students complete the rest of the second body paragraph individually, based on their own research. Circulate around the room to ensure students are on task.

10. Introduce the essay graphic organizer and explain to students that they will use the information from the claim-evidence graphic organizer to write their essay. Tell students that they should start

writing their introduction by using the information in the top block. If possible, model the process with the aid of a projector.

11. For the first body paragraph, tell students that they will use the information in the explanation field first, including the transition word, followed by the corresponding textual evidence from their source (website, magazine, book, etc.). Model the process for the first explanation with the aid of a projector, if possible. Explain to students that they will repeat this sequence for each explanation. You may wish to have students use colored pencils or highlighters to color-code the graphic organizer.

12. Have students complete the first body paragraph individually. Circulate and provide assistance, as necessary.

13. Explain to students that they will follow the same process for the second body paragraph. Have them complete the second body paragraph about disadvantages using the information in the claim-evidence graphic organizer.

14. *Exit ticket:* Ask students to complete the color-coding practice activity #2.

Assessment

- *Formative:* Assess students' ability to support their opinions/claims with specific examples and textual evidence.
- *Summative:* Assess students' ability to write explanatory essays using the features of academic writing (e.g., topic sentence, explanation, transition words, textual evidence).

FIGURE 5.13

Color-Coding Practice Activity #1

Color the following sentences using the appropriate colors for the topic sentence, transition words, explanation, and evidence from text.

Technology affects our lives every day. Like everything, technology has both advantages and disadvantages.

First, technology affects our lives in a positive way because we can communicate with each other faster. According to the text, "Instead of writing and mailing a letter, people can send an email from their computers." However, if people use computers too much, they don't have time to talk to their friends face to face. Based on the text, "They worry about how much time people spend using their cell phones and computers instead of talking to their friends."

FIGURE 5.14

Color-Coding Practice Activity #2

Name: _____   **Date:** _____

Color-code the following text:

Technology has a positive impact on our lives because we can get where we want quicker. Based on the text, "They can get to work or school easily by driving a car or taking a bus." Cars and buses can have a negative impact on people's health and the environment by causing illnesses and more pollution. According to the text, "Instead of relying on cars and buses, people should walk or ride a bike because this is better for their health or the environment."

Lesson 10: Creating Opening Statements

Lesson at a Glance: In groups, students will prepare for a debate by writing an opening statement using a graphic organizer. Students will practice transition words for adding information (*also, in addition, furthermore*) and contrasting information (*however, on the other hand*) that will be used in the debate.

Time Frame: two 75-minute periods

Materials

- T-notes graphic organizer (Figure 1.9)
- Opening statement graphic organizer (Figure 1.11)
- *Optional:* Computer/projector
- *Optional:* Rebuttal table tent (Figure 1.12)

Preparation

1. Display the following objectives and SEL foci on a whiteboard, chart paper, or slide presentation:
   - **Content Objective:** Create an opening statement for debating whether technology makes our lives better or worse.
   - **Language Objective:** Justify opinions about the impact of technology using sentence stems orally and in writing.
   - **SEL Foci:** Respect for others, teamwork
   - **CCSS Standard:** CCSS.ELA-LITERACY.SL.9-10.1.B: Work with peers to set rules for collegial discussions and decision making (e.g., informal consensus, taking votes on key issues, presentation of alternate views), clear goals and deadlines, and individual roles as needed.
   - **CCSS Standard** (*optional: aligned with Step 6*): CCSS.ELA-LITERACY.SL.9-10.5: Make strategic use of digital media (e.g., textual, graphical, audio, visual, and interactive elements) in

presentations to enhance understanding of findings, reasoning, and evidence and to add interest.

2. Prepare the necessary materials.

3. Create your agenda using the following lesson activities.

4. Ensure that the seating arrangement enables students to work in groups.

Activities

1. *Do-now activity:* Write or display the following question and sentence stem on the board. Ask students to "turn and talk" to a partner by asking and responding to the question orally. Select a few students to share out with the whole class.

   What is your opinion about technology? Does it make our lives better or worse? Why?

   In my opinion, technology makes our lives _____ because _____.

   Tell students that today they will be preparing for their big debate!

2. Discuss the content objective, language objective, and SEL foci with students.

3. Ask students to review the T-notes graphic organizer they filled out in Lesson 1. Explain that they will now join either the pro team or the con team. The pro team will explain the advantages of technology and argue that it makes our lives better, and the con team will explain the disadvantages of technology and argue that it makes our lives worse. (Note: You may want to preselect the teams to ensure that they are roughly equal in size.)

4. Model how to complete the opening statement graphic organizer by completing the first few lines orally. Then break students into the pro and con teams and have each team complete the graphic organizer as a group. Circulate to help students, as needed, as well as to ensure that all students are assigned a part of the opening statement. Once teams have finished, they can practice their

pronunciation by reading their statement aloud. Note: Depending on your class size, students may need to team up to share ideas from the opening statement graphic organizer. Typically, students prepare one or two sentences each.

5. *Exit ticket:* Have students illustrate one or two main points from their team's opening statement.

6. *Optional:* Have students create visuals to accompany their opening statement. Although this step is optional, it is a great resource for helping the opposing team understand and rebut the other team's points. Consider having students use a computer program to create a visual slide to accompany their presentation. There should not be any writing on the slide—just images to support their statements. For example, if the team mentions that technology facilitates communication, they might show images of families and friends communicating via smartphone or laptop. Alternatively, if they explain how distracting cell phones can be, they might show images of people talking on the phone while driving.

Assessment

- *Formative:* Assess students' ability to justify their opinions/claims using textual evidence by completing the opening statement graphic organizer.
- *Formative:* Assess students' ability to link similar ideas using transition words (*also, in addition, furthermore*) and opposing ideas using transition words (*however, on the other hand*).

Lesson 11: Preparing for the Debate

Lesson at a Glance: In groups, students will prepare for debate by practicing the rebuttal phase of the debate using a write-around activity. Students will prepare for the closing statements of the debate using sentence frames.

Time Frame: three 75-minute periods

Materials

- Lined paper with prepared sentences for write-around activity
- Transitions practice activity (Figure 5.15)
- T-notes graphic organizer (Figure 1.9)
- Opening statement graphic organizer (Figure 1.11)
- Rebuttal table tent (Figure 1.12)
- Closing statement table tent (Figure 1.13)
- Debate rubric (Figure 1.16)
- *Optional:* Computer/projector

Preparation

1. Display the following objectives and SEL foci on a whiteboard, chart paper, or slide presentation:
   - **Content Objective:** Summarize main ideas for debating whether technology makes our lives better or worse.
   - **Language Objective:** Justify opinions about the impact of technology using textual evidence and sentence stems orally and in writing.
   - **SEL Foci:** Respect for others, appreciating diversity
   - **CCSS Standard:** CCSS.ELA-LITERACY.SL.9-10.1.D: Respond thoughtfully to diverse perspectives, summarize points of agreement and disagreement, and, when warranted, qualify or justify their own views and understanding and make new connections in light of the evidence and reasoning presented.

2. Prepare the necessary materials.

3. Create your agenda using the following lesson activities.

4. Ensure that the seating arrangement enables students to participate in the write-around activity. Ideally, students will be seated in a circle.

5. Prepare for the write-around activity by writing the following sentences on four different sheets of lined paper. One sentence should go at the top of each paper:

   - Technology makes our lives better by letting us communicate with people who live far away.
   - Technology makes our lives better by making it easier to find information quickly.
   - Technology makes our lives worse because it is distracting.
   - Technology makes our lives worse because it is dangerous.

Activities

1. *Do-now activity:* Have students complete the transition words practice activity.

2. Discuss the content objective, language objective, and SEL foci with students.

3. Introduce the rebuttal sentence stems: "I disagree with what you said about _____. However, I believe _____." Remind students of the transition words that they have practiced so far, including words for adding information (*also, in addition, furthermore*) and words for contrasting information (*however, on the other hand*). Remind students of the language for agreement and disagreement that they have been practicing: (*I agree, I disagree*).

4. Post and explain the debate rubric and debate scoring template. Use native language support if necessary. Explain that all students must participate in all three parts of the debate.

5. Provide each team with a copy of the opposing team's opening statement so they can refer to it during the practice.

6. Explain to students that they are going to prepare for the rebuttal phase of the debate by participating in a write-around activity. Show students the four papers with the sentences on the top. Model the activity for students. Show students (using a projector, if possible) the paper that says, "Technology makes our lives better by letting us communicate with people who live far away." Tell students they have two options. They can write "I agree. Also, I believe . . ." or "I disagree. However, I believe . . . ." Elicit students' input to model using the answer stems.

7. Engage students in the write-around activity. Students will write a sentence and pass the paper to the right. Continue until everyone has written at least four sentences. As the papers are circulated, students add their responses using the sentence stems. (Note: Depending on your class size, you may want to create more sheets of paper to circulate. Alternatively, you can have students do the activity in pairs.)

8. Once everyone is done, have them share out. Explain that this is similar to the rebuttal phase of the upcoming debate.

9. Explain to students that now it is time to prepare for closing statements—the final phase of the debate. Tell students that in this phase, they should not introduce any new information. Instead, they should summarize their most important ideas. This is their last chance to convince the judge(s). Tell students that they should use transition words for the closing statements. They can choose between *as you can see* and *to sum up*. Model closing statements for both the pro and con teams. Explain that they can summarize what they wrote in their opening statements.

10. *Exit ticket:* Tell students to prepare a closing statement in their notebooks. Have them show their completed sentences.

11. *Optional lesson extension activity:* Have students prepare for the debate by practicing their opening statements, rebuttal sentences, and closing statements.

Assessment

- *Formative:* Assess students' ability to link similar ideas using transition words (*also, in addition, furthermore*) and opposing ideas using transition words (*however, on the other hand*)
- *Formative:* Assess students' ability to create a conclusion statement using transition words (*as you can see, to sum up*).

FIGURE 5.15

Transition Words Practice Activity

Name: _____   **Date:** _____

Complete the paragraph using the following transition words:

Also	*In addition*	*However*

Cell phones are making our lives worse because they are very dangerous. _____, they are distracting. _____, people spend too much time using their phones instead of talking to people face-to-face. _____, there are some advantages to cell phones. For example, you can make calls in an emergency and communicate with people who live far away.

Lesson 12: Debate

Lesson at a Glance: In groups, students will debate the issue of whether technology makes our lives better or worse. They will participate in all three phases of the debate: opening statements, rebuttal, and closing statements.

Time Frame: one or two 75-minute time periods

Materials

- Student notebooks or binders
- T-notes graphic organizer (Figure 1.9)
- Opening statement graphic organizers (pro and con teams) (Figure 1.11)
- Closing statement table tent (Figure 1.13)
- Rebuttal table tent (Figure 1.12)
- Debate scoring template (Figure 1.14)
- Debate rubric (Figure 1.16)
- *Optional:* Computer/projector

Preparation

1. Display the following objectives and SEL foci on a whiteboard, chart paper, or slide presentation:
   - **Content Objective:** Debate whether technology makes our lives better or worse.
   - **Language Objective:** Argue about the impact of technology by stating points and counterpoints in a debate using reasoning and evidence.
   - **SEL Foci:** Respect for others, appreciating diversity
   - **CCSS Standard:** CCSS.ELA-LITERACY.SL.9-10.1.D: Respond thoughtfully to diverse perspectives, summarize points of agreement and disagreement, and, when warranted, qualify or justify their own views and understanding and make new connections in light of the evidence and reasoning presented.

2. Prepare the necessary materials.

3. Create your agenda using the following lesson activities.

4. Ensure that the seating arrangement enables students to participate in a whole-class debate. Ideally, students will sit in two opposing rows that face each other.

5. *Optional:* If students created visuals to accompany their presentations, project them using the projector.

6. *Optional:* Invite a third party to be the judge of the debate. This could be an administrator, counselor, or another teacher. Having a guest judge eliminates any discomfort for the classroom teacher, as by now it is difficult to be impartial and most likely you'll want to have a tie! In addition, students often feel proud to showcase their work for the guest. If you opt to do this, we recommend doing a practice run of the debate from start to finish the day prior so students know exactly what to expect before the big day.

Activities

1. *Do-now activity:* Post the following rule on the board: *We disagree with ideas, not people.* Ask students to reflect on this statement using one of these sentence stems: "This sentence means _____" or "This sentence is important because _____." Have students share out.

2. Review the content objective, language objective, and SEL foci with students.

3. Remind students of the expectations for the debate by posting the debate rubric and debate scoring template. Use native language support if necessary. Remind students that everyone must participate in all three parts of the debate.

4. Allow students five minutes in their groups to prepare for their opening statements. During this time, ensure that they are seated in the order they're slated to speak, practice their pronunciation, and consult their notes.

5. Hold the debate. Flip a coin to determine which side begins. As students present their opening statements, ensure the opposing team is listening and taking notes to prepare for the rebuttal. Use the debate rubric and debate scoring template (if no third-party judge is present) to assess student performance on the debate. After both teams present their opening statements, transition to the rebuttal phase.

6. For the rebuttal phase, pass out copies of the rebuttal table tent. Encourage all students to speak and to use the table tent. Tell students they can consult their notes, but they should not read them verbatim. (Note: You can allot a specific time frame for the rebuttal, or you can wait until the back-and-forth comes to a natural end before moving on.)

7. When the rebuttal phase ends, it is time for the closing statements. Collect the rebuttal table tent and pass out the closing statement table tent. Whichever team went second during opening statements should go first for closing statements. Encourage all students to speak and to use the table tent. Remind students that they can consult their notes, but they should not read them verbatim.

8. *Exit ticket:* Share feedback based on the debate scoring template with students. Give students time to reflect on the experience of participating in an academic debate. Consider asking the following reflection questions:
   - What did you like about the debate?
   - What would you change?
   - What was easy for you?
   - What was difficult?
   - What did you learn from this activity?

Assessment

- *Summative:* Assess students' ability to justify their opinions/claims on the impact of technology using the debate rubric.

References

Alvarez, E. (2020, February 3). *Long Island bilingual/ENL coordinators' meeting* [Slide deck]. New York State Department of Education. https://www.esboces.org/site/handlers/filedownload.ashx?moduleinstanceid=4985&dataid=17353&FileName=LI%20Presentation%20Elisa%20Alvarez-OBEWL.pdf

Barba, Y. C., Newcombe, A., Ruiz, R., & Cordero, N. (2019). Building bridges for new immigrant students through asset-based consultation. *Contemporary School Psychology, 23,* 31–46.

Benseman, J. (2014). Adult refugee learners with limited literacy: Needs and effective responses. *Refuge, 30*(1), 93–103.

Birman, D., & Tran, N. (2017). When worlds collide: Academic adjustment of Somali Bantu students with limited formal education in a U.S. elementary school. *International Journal of Intercultural Relations, 60,* 132–144.

Bloom, B. S. (1956). *Taxonomy of educational objectives: The classification of educational goals.* Longmans, Green.

Boston Children's Hospital. (2019). Refugee and immigrants core stressors toolkit. https://redcap.tch.harvard.edu/redcap_edc/surveys/?s=RCDFFHWK4P7THRL4

Bowers, E., Fitts, S., Quirk, M., & Jung, W. (2010). Effective strategies for developing academic English: Professional development and teacher practices. *Bilingual Research Journal, 33*(1), 95–110.

Brown, H. D. (2007). *Principles of language learning and teaching* (5th ed.). Pearson Education.

Bruner, J. S. (1960). *The process of education.* Harvard University Press.

Calderón, M. (2011). *Teaching reading & comprehension to English learners K–5.* Solution Tree.

Cartwright, C., & Filimon, N. (2018). Writing with colors: A strategy for students with limited or interrupted formal education (SLIFE). *MATSOL Currents, 39*(1), 41–43.

Cashiola, L., & Potter, D. (2020). *Long-term English learners (LTELs): Predictors, patterns, & outcomes, defining LTEL (Part 1).* Rice University, Kinder Institute for Urban Research. https://kinder.rice.edu/research/long-term-english-learners-ltels-predictors-patterns-outcomes-brief-1-defining-ltel

Chamot, A. U., Keatley, C. W., & Anstrom, K. (2013). *Keys to learning.* Pearson Longman.

Cofer, J. O. (1995). *An island like you: Stories of the barrio.* Puffin Books.

Cohan, A., & Honigsfeld, A. (2017). Students with interrupted formal education (SIFEs): Actionable practices. *NABE Journal of Research and Practice, 8*(1), 166–175.

Collaborative for Academic, Social, and Emotional Learning (CASEL). (2017). *Sample teaching activities to support core competencies of social and emotional learning.* https://casel.

org/sample-teaching-activities-to-support-core-competencies *CASEL'S SEL framework.* https://casel.org/core-competencies

Collaborative for Academic, Social, and Emotional Learning (CASEL). (2020). What is the CASEL framework? https://casel.org/fundamentals-of-sel/what-is-the-casel-framework

Collins, T., & Maples, M. (2008). *Gateway to science.* Thomson Heinle.

Cotterall, S., & Cohen, R. (2003). Scaffolding for second language writers: Producing an academic essay. *ELT Journal, 57*(2), 158–166.

Creagh, S. (2019). Reading pedagogy for refugee-background young people learning literacy for the first time in English as an additional language. *European Journal of Applied Linguistics and TEFL, 8*(1), 3–20.

Custodio, B., & O'Loughlin, J. B. (2020). Students with interrupted formal education: Understanding who they are. *American Educator, 44*(1), 9–11.

Daly, P. (2012). *The essence of innovation: Uncovering the conditions essential for innovative instructional practice* [Doctoral dissertation]. ProQuest Dissertations.

Darling-Hammond, L., & Cook-Harvey, C. M. (2018). *Educating the whole child: Improving school climate to support student success.* Learning Policy Institute.

DeCapua, A. (2016). Reaching students with limited or interrupted formal education through culturally responsive teaching. *Language and Linguistics Compass, 10*(5), 225–237.

DeCapua, A., & Marshall, H. W. (2010). Serving ELLs with limited or interrupted education: Intervention that works. *TESOL Journal, 1,* 49–70.

DeCapua, A., & Marshall, H. W. (2011a). *Breaking new ground: Teaching students with limited or interrupted formal education in U.S. secondary schools.* University of Michigan Press.

DeCapua, A., & Marshall, H. W. (2011b). Reaching ELLs at risk: Instruction for students with limited or interrupted formal education. *Preventing School Failure, 55*(1), 35–41.

DeCapua, A., & Marshall, H.W. (2015). Reframing the conversation about students with limited or interrupted formal education: From achievement gap to cultural dissonance. *NASSP Bulletin, 99*(1), 356–370.

DeCapua, A., Smathers, W., & Tang, L. F. (2007). Schooling, interrupted. *Educational Leadership, 64*(6), 40–46.

DeCapua, A., Smathers, W., & Tang, L. F. (2009). *Meeting the needs of students with limited or interrupted schooling: A guide for educators.* University of Michigan Press.

DelliCarpini, M. (2012). Success with ELLs: We are all writers! Building second language writing skills in the ELA classroom. *The English Journal, 101*(5), 97–101.

Digby, S. (2019). *Supporting Latino students with interrupted formal education: A guide for teachers.* The K–12 Outreach Program, Institute of Latin American Studies, Columbia University.

Duran, E., Gusman, J., & Shefelbine, J. (2005a). *ACCESS to math.* Great Source Education Group.

Duran, E., Gusman, J., & Shefelbine, J. (2005b). *ACCESS to science.* Great Source Education Group.

Dutro, S., & Kinsella, K. (2010). English language development: Issues and implementation in grades 6–12. In *Improving education for English learners: Research-based approaches.* California Department of Education.

Echevarría, J., Vogt, M. E., & Short, D. (2004). *Making content comprehensible for English learners: The SIOP model* (2nd ed.). Pearson.

Echevarría, J., Vogt, M. E., & Short, D. (2014). *Making content comprehensible for secondary English learners: The SIOP model.* Pearson.

Fagan, D., & Herrera, L. (2022). Supporting English learners with disabilities. *State Education Standard, 22*(1), 26–31.

Fenner, D. S. (2013). Implementing the Common Core State Standards for English learners: The changing role of the ESL teacher. In *A Summary of the TESOL International Association Convening.*

Filimon, N. (2023). *Using an instructional protocol to increase the literacy achievement of secondary students with limited or interrupted formal education (SLIFE)* [Doctoral dissertation]. ProQuest Dissertations.

Freeman, Y., & Freeman, D. (2002). *Closing the achievement gap: How to reach limited-formal-schooling and long-term English learners*. Heinemann.

Genesee, F., Lindholm-Leary, K., Saunders, W., & Christian, D. (2006). *Educating English language learners*. Cambridge University Press.

Giouroukakis, V., & Honigsfeld, A. (2010). High-stakes testing and English Language Learners: Using culturally and linguistically responsive literacy practices in the high school English classroom. *TESOL Journal, 1*(4), 470–499.

Goldenberg, C. (2011). Reading instruction for English language learners. In M. L. Kamil, P. D. Pearson, E. B. Moje, & P. P. Afflerbach (Eds.), *Handbook of reading research* (Vol. 4, pp. 684–710). Routledge.

González, N., Moll, L. C., & Amanti, C. (Eds.). (2005). *Funds of knowledge: Theorizing practices in households, communities, and classrooms*. Lawrence Erlbaum Associates.

Gottlieb, M. (2016). *Assessing English language learners: Bridges from language proficiency to academic achievement* (2nd ed.). Corwin.

Hess, K. (2004). Applying Webb's Depth-of-Knowledge (DOK) levels in reading. *NCIEA*. http://www.nciea.org/publications/DOKreading_KH08.pdf.

Hess, K. (2005). Applying Webb's Depth-of-Knowledge (DOK) levels in writing. *NCIEA*. http://www.nciea.org/publications/DOKwriting_KH08.pdf.

Hess, K., Jones, B., Carlock, D., and Walkup, J. (2009). Cognitive rigor: Blending the strengths of Bloom's taxonomy and Webb's depth of knowledge to enhance classroom-level processes. http://www.standardsco.com/PDF /Cognitive_Rigor_Paper.pdf

Hill, R., & Hall, C. O (2012). *Just add water*. Water for South Sudan.

Honig, B., Diamond, L., Gutlohn, L., & Cole, C. L. (2008). *Teaching reading sourcebook* (2nd ed.). Arena.

Hos, R. (2016). Caring is not enough: Teachers' enactment of ethical care for adolescent students with limited or interrupted formal education (SLIFE) in a newcomer classroom. *Education and Urban Society, 48*(5), 479–503.

Hos, R., Murray-Johnson, K., & Correia, A. (2019). Cultivating capital for high school newcomers: A case study of an urban newcomer classroom. *Journal of Ethnic and Cultural Studies, 6*(1), 101–116.

Institute of Education Sciences. (2018). The right fit: Selecting an English learning program for your students. https://ies.ed.gov/ncee/edlabs/infographics/pdf/REL_NW_The_Right_Fit.pdf

Kennedy, A. A., & Lamina, P. (2016). The role of ambiguity tolerance in the development of literacy skills of secondary students with limited or interrupted formal education (SLIFE). *Reading in Virginia, 38*, 71–78.

Kim, J., Olson, C. B., Scarcella, R., Kramer, J., Pearson, M., van Dyk, D., . . . & Land, R. (2011). A randomized experiment of a cognitive strategies approach to text-based analytical writing for mainstreamed Latino English language learners in grades 6 to 12. *Journal of Research on Educational Effectiveness, 4*, 231–263.

Kinsella, K. (2005). Teaching academic vocabulary. *Aiming high: Sonoma County Office of Education*. https://www.scoe.org/docs/ah/AH_kinsella2.pdf

Kinsella, K., & Feldman, K. (2005). *Narrowing the language gap: The case for explicit vocabulary instruction*. Scholastic.

Lee, S. (2018). Scaffolding evidence-based writing for English learners in three steps. *The Reading Teacher, 72*(1), 99–106.

Lemov, D. (2016). *Reading reconsidered: A practical guide to rigorous literacy instruction*. Jossey-Bass.

Li, X., & Zhang, M. (2004). Why Mei still cannot read and what can be done. *Journal of Adolescent and Adult Literacy, 48*(2), 92–101.

Manspile, E., Atwell, M., & Bridgeland, J. (2021). *Immigrant students and English learners: Challenges faced in high school and postsecondary education.* Civic.

Massachusetts Department of Elementary and Secondary Education. (2016). *ESL: Access to clean water.* https://www.doe.mass.edu/ele/instruction/mcu/eslg7-clean-water.docx

Massachusetts Department of Elementary and Secondary Education. (2019). *Social and emotional learning & culturally responsive teaching reflection guide.* https://www.doe.mass.edu/edeval/implementation/

Massachusetts Department of Elementary and Secondary Education. (2022a). *ESL best practices quick reference guide: Newcomers.* https://www.doe.mass.edu/ele/esl-toolkit/tools-resources/best-practices/newcomers.docx

Massachusetts Department of Elementary and Secondary Education. (2022b). *ESL best practices quick reference guide: Students with limited or interrupted formal education (SLIFE).* https://www.doe.mass.edu/ele/esl-toolkit/tools-resources/best-practices/slife.docx

Menken, K. (2013). Emergent bilingual students in secondary school: Along the academic language and literacy continuum. *Language Teaching, 46*(4), 438–476.

Menken, K., & Kleyn, T. (2009, April). The difficult road for long-term English learners. *Educational Leadership, 66*(7). https://www.ascd.org/el/articles/the-difficult-road-for-long-term-english-learners

Montero, M. K., Newmaster, S., & Ledger, S. (2014). Exploring early reading instructional strategies to advance the print literacy development of adolescent SLIFE. *Journal of Adolescent and Adult Literacy, 58*(1), 59–69.

National Governors Association Center for Best Practices, Council of Chief State School Officers. (2010). *Common Core State Standards for English language arts and literacy in history/social studies, science, and technical subjects.* https://corestandards.org/wp-content/uploads/2023/09/ELA_Standards1.pdf

Olsen, L. (2014). Meeting the unique needs of long term English learners: A guide for educators. *National Education Association.* https://calauthorizers.org/wp-content/uploads/2020/11/Copy-of-LongTermEngLangLearner-NEA.pdf

Olsen, L., & Jaramillo, A. (1999). *Turning the tides of exclusion: A guide for educators and advocates for immigrant students.* California Tomorrow.

Olson, C. B., Kim, J. S., Scarcella, R., Kramer, J., Pearson, M., Van Dyk, D., . . . & Land, R. E. (2012). Enhancing the interpretive reading and analytical writing of mainstreamed English learners in secondary school: Results from a randomized field trial using a cognitive strategies approach. *American Educational Research Journal, 4,* 323–355.

Olson, C. B., Land, R., Anselmi, T., & Aubuchon, C. (2011). Teaching secondary English learners to understand, analyze, and write interpretive essays about theme. *Journal of Adolescent & Adult Literacy, 54*(4), 245–256.

Olson, C. B., Matuchniak, T., Chung, H. Q., Stumpf, R., & Farkas, G. (2017). Reducing achievement gaps in academic writing for Latinos and English learners in grades 7–12. *Journal of Educational Psychology, 109*(1), 1–21.

Olson, C. B., Scarcella, R., & Matuchniak, T. (2015). English learners, writing, and the Common Core. *The Elementary School Journal, 115*(4), 570–592.

O'Toole, T. (2015). *Writing with colors.* [Professional development workshop]. Lawrence High School.

Perez, Z. P. (2014). Removing barriers to higher education for undocumented students. *Center for American Progress.* https://www.luminafoundation.org/files/resources/removing-barriers-for-undocumented-students.pdf

Potochnick, S. (2018). The academic adaptation of immigrant students with interrupted schooling. *American Educational Research Journal, 55*(4), 859–892.

Reading League & National Committee for Effective Literacy. (2023, March). Joint statement: Understanding the difference: The science of reading and implementation for English learners/emergent bilinguals (ELs/EBs). *The Reading League.* https://www.

thereadingleague.org/wp-content/uploads/2023/10/Joint-Statement-on-the-Science-of-Reading-and-English-Learners_Emergent-Bilinguals-20.pdf

Rishel, T. (2018). *Research in stress and coping in education*. Information Age.

Rose, D. (2017). Languages of schooling: Embedding literacy learning with genre-based pedagogy. *European Journal of Applied Linguistics, 5*(2), 1–31.

Ruiz de Velasco, J., & Fix, M. (2000). Overlooked and underserved: Immigrant students in US secondary schools. *Urban Institute Report*. The Urban Institute.

Schifini, A. (1997). Reading instruction for the pre-literate and struggling older students. *Scholastic Literacy Research Paper, 3*(13). Scholastic.

Schleppegrell, M. J. (2001). Linguistic features of the language of schooling. *Linguistics and Education, 12*(4), 431–459.

Short, D. J., & Boyson, B. A. (2012). *Helping newcomer students succeed in secondary school and beyond*. Center for Applied Linguistics.

Symons, C., & Bian, Y. (2022). Exploring a linguistic orientation to facilitating refugee-background youth's meaning-making with texts: A self-study. *Linguistics and Education, 70*, 1–15.

Tigert, J. M., Peercy, M. M., Fredricks, D., & Kidwell, T. (2021). Humanizing classroom management as a core practice for teachers of multilingual students. *TESOL Quarterly, 56*(4), 1087–1111.

Umansky, I., Hopkins, M., Dabach, D. B., Porter, L., Thompson, K., & Pompa, D. (2018). *Understanding and supporting the educational needs of recently arrived immigrant English learner students: Lessons for state and local education agencies*. Council of Chief State School Officers. https://ccsso.org/resource-library/understanding-and-supporting-educational-needs-recently-arrived-immigrant-english

U.S. Department of Education. (2023). *Newcomer toolkit*. National Clearinghouse for English Language Acquisition. https://ncela.ed.gov/educator-support/toolkits/newcomer-toolkit

Watkins, E., & Liu, K. (2013). Who are English language learners with disabilities? *Impact, 26*(1). https://publications.ici.umn.edu/impact/26-1/who-are-english-language-learners-with-disabilities

Webb, N. (1997). *Research monograph number 6: Criteria for alignment of expectations and assessments on mathematics and science education*. Council of Chief State School Officers.

WIDA. (2015). *Focus on SLIFE: Students with limited or interrupted formal education*. https://wida.wisc.edu/sites/default/files/resource/FocusOn-SLIFE.pdf

WIDA. (2020). *WIDA English language development standards framework, 2020 edition: Kindergarten–grade 12*. Board of Regents of the University of Wisconsin System.

WIDA. (2023). *ACCESS for ELLs: Interpretive guide for score reports: Grades K–12*. https://wida.wisc.edu/sites/default/files/resource/Interpretive-Guide.pdf

Wiggins, G., & McTighe, J. (2005). *Understanding by design* (2nd ed.). ASCD.

Wilson, B. (2021). *Wilson Reading System* (4th ed.). Wilson Language Training Corporation.

Windle, J., & Miller, J. (2012). Approaches to teaching low literacy refugee-background students. *Australian Journal of Language and Literacy, 35*(3), 317–333.

Windle, J., & Miller, J. (2019). Scaffolding second language literacy: A model for students with interrupted schooling. *European Journal of Applied Linguistics and TEFL, 8*(1), 39–59.

Wright, W. E. (2015). *Foundations for teaching English language learners: Research, theory, policy, and practice* (2nd ed.). Caslon.

Zong, J., & Batalova, J. (2019). How many unauthorized immigrants graduate from U.S. high schools annually? *Migration Policy Institute*. https://www.migrationpolicy.org/research/unauthorized-immigrants-graduate-us-high-schools

Zwiers, J., & Crawford, M. (2011). *Academic conversations: Classroom talk that fosters critical thinking and coherent understandings*. Stenhouse.

Zwiers, J., O'Hara, S., & Pritchard, R. (2014). *Common core standards in diverse classrooms: Essential practices for developing academic language and disciplinary literacy*. Stenhouse.

Index

The letter *f* following a page locator denotes a figure.

About the Authors

 **Nicoleta Filimon** has been a teacher, dean of curriculum and instruction, assistant principal, education consultant, and teacher educator for almost two decades. She has taught ESL/ELD to MLs and SLIFE for more than 13 years in Massachusetts. Since 2006, she has presented on the subject of educating MLs and SLIFE locally, regionally, and internationally. Nicoleta is the recipient of several awards, including the University of Massachusetts Lowell (UMASS Lowell) Outstanding Dissertation in Practice Award (2023), MATSOL Teacher of the Year Award (2018), Sontag Prize in Urban Education (2013, 2014, 2015, 2016, 2017), and the Haverty Scholar in Education Award (2007). She recently received her doctorate in leadership in schooling from UMASS Lowell. A multilingual learner herself, Nicoleta is originally from Romania.

 **Christi Cartwright-Lacerda** has been an ESL/ELD teacher of MLs and SLIFE for the past 10 years. She is the recipient of several awards, including the Rising Star Teacher of the Year Award from her school district (2018), NoVo Foundation SEL Innovation Fund Award (2018), Sontag Prize in Urban Education (2017, 2021, 2022, 2023), and the MATSOL Linda Schulman Innovation Fund Award (2018, 2020). She has presented on the subject of social-emotional learning for MLs and strategies for educating MLs and SLIFE locally, regionally, and internationally since 2015. Christi also works as an education consultant, sharing instructional strategies for newcomer MLs and SLIFE.

Related ASCD Resources: Multilingual Learners

At the time of publication, the following resources were available (ASCD stock numbers in parentheses).

Dispelling Misconceptions About English Language Learners: Research-Based Ways to Improve Instruction by Barbara Gottschalk (#120010)

The Language-Rich Classroom: A Research-Based Framework for Teaching English Language Learners by Pérsida Himmele & William Himmele (#108037)

Learning in a New Language: A Schoolwide Approach to Support K–8 Emergent Bilinguals by Lori Helman (#120015)

Literacy Strong All Year Long: Powerful Lessons for Grades K–2, 2nd Edition by Valerie Ellery, Lori Oczkus, & Timothy Rasinski (#118046)

Planning Effective Instruction for ELLs (Quick Reference Guide) by Pérsida Himmele & William Himmele (#QRG119029)

Restoring Students' Innate Power: Trauma-Responsive Strategies for Teaching Multilingual Newcomers by Louise El Yaafouri (#122004)

Teaching English Language Learners Across the Content Areas by Judie Haynes & Debbie Zacarian (#109032)

Tools for Teaching Writing: Strategies and Interventions for Diverse Learners in Grades 3–8 by David Campos & Kathleen Fad (#114051)

For up-to-date information about ASCD resources, go to www.ascd.org. You can search the complete archives of *Educational Leadership* at www.ascd.org/el.

For more information, send an email to member@ascd.org; call 1-800-933-2723 or 703-578-9600; send a fax to 703-575-5400; or write to Information Services, ASCD, 2800 Shirlington Road, Suite 1001, Arlington, Virginia USA.